Great Americans of History

THOMAS JEFFERSON

A Character Sketch

EDWARD S. ELLIS

with supplementary essay by G. MERCER ADAM
with an account of the Louisiana Purchase together with
anecdotes, characteristics, and chronology

Thomas Jefferson

Edward S. Ellis

© 1st World Library – Literary Society, 2004
PO Box 2211
Fairfield, IA 52556
www.1stworldlibrary.org
First Edition

LCCN: 2005902136

Softcover ISBN: 1-59540-825-8
Hardcover ISBN: 1-59540-824-X
eBook ISBN: 1-59540-826-6

Purchase *"Thomas Jefferson"*
as a traditional bound book at:
www.1stWorldLibrary.org/purchase.asp?ISBN=

1st World Library Literary Society is a nonprofit organization dedicated to promoting literacy by:

- Creating a free internet library accessible from any computer worldwide.
- Hosting writing competitions and offering book publishing scholarships.

**Readers interested in supporting literacy through sponsorship, donations or membership please contact:
literacy@1stworldlibrary.org
Check us out at: www.1stworldlibrary.ORG
and start downloading free ebooks today.**

Thomas Jefferson
*contributed by Logan & Jason
in support of
1st World Library Literary Society*

"It is the duty of every good citizen to use all the opportunities which occur to him, for preserving documents relating to the history of our country."

- Thomas Jefferson, letter to Hugh P. Taylor

To our father Bill Krochalis:

Father of mine, you have taught me, not only how to learn, but how to love and appreciate my studies. Herodotus to you, and now you to me, father of mine, father of history. You amaze me, daddy, because you will not tell me your expectations, but rather, you exemplify a brilliant mind, and I am encouraged and enlightened by your passion for thought. I know you love me because by increasing my knowledge, you have set me free.

- Logan

Dad you are my confidant, my coach, my best audience, my toughest teacher, my favorite ski buddy, my reality check and my dearest companion, your belief in me is the foundation I built upon. Thank you.

- Jason

"Enlighten the people, generally, and tyranny and oppressions of body and mind will vanish like spirits at the dawn of day."

- Thomas Jefferson, letter to Dupont de Nemours

No golden eagle, warm from the stamping press of the mint, is more sharply impressed with its image and superscription than was the formative period of our government by the genius and personality of Thomas Jefferson.

Standing on the threshold of the nineteenth century, no one who attempted to peer down the shadowy vista, saw more clearly than he the possibilities, the perils, the pitfalls and the achievements that were within the grasp of the Nation. None was inspired by purer patriotism. None was more sagacious, wise and prudent, and none understood his countrymen better.

By birth an aristocrat, by nature he was a democrat. The most learned man that ever sat in the president's chair, his tastes were the simple ones of a farmer. Surrounded by the pomp and ceremony of Washington and Adams' courts, his dress was homely. He despised titles, and preferred severe plainness of speech and the sober garb of the Quakers.

"What is the date of your birth, Mr. President?" asked an admirer.

"Of what possible concern is that to you?" queried the President in turn.

"We wish to give it fitting celebration."

"For that reason, I decline to enlighten you; nothing could be more distasteful to me than what you propose, and, when you address me, I shall be obliged if you will omit the 'Mr.'"

If we can imagine Washington doing so undignified a thing as did President Lincoln, when he first met our present Secretary of State, (John Sherman) and compared their respective heights by standing back to back, a sheet of paper resting on the crowns of Washington and Jefferson would have lain horizontal and been six feet two inches from the earth, but the one was magnificent in physique, of massive frame and prodigious strength,—the other was thin, wiry, bony, active, but with muscles of steel, while both were as straight as the proverbial Indian arrow.

Jefferson's hair was of sandy color, his cheeks ruddy, his eyes of a light hazel, his features angular, but glowing with intelligence and neither could lay any claim to the gift of oratory.

Washington lacked literary ability, while in the hand of Jefferson, the pen was as masterful as the sword in the clutch of Saladin or Godfrey of Bouillon. Washington had only a common school education, while Jefferson was a classical scholar and could express his thoughts in excellent Italian, Spanish and French, and both were masters of their temper.

Jefferson was an excellent violinist, a skilled mathematician and a profound scholar. Add to all these his spotless integrity and honor, his statesmanship, and his well curbed but aggressive patriotism, and he embodied within himself all the attributes of an ideal president of the United States.

In the colonial times, Virginia was the South and Massachusetts the North. The other colonies were only appendages. The New York Dutchman dozed over his beer and pipe, and when the other New England settlements saw the Narragansetts bearing down upon them with upraised tomahawks, they ran for cover and yelled to Massachusetts to save them.

Clayborne fired popguns at Lord Baltimore, and the Catholic and Protestant Marylanders enacted Toleration Acts, and then chased one another over the border, with some of the fugitives running all the way to the Carolinas, where the settlers were perspiring over their efforts in installing new governors and thrusting them out again, in the hope that a half-fledged statesman would turn up sometime or other in the shuffle.

What a roystering set those Cavaliers were! Fond of horse racing, cock fighting, gambling and drinking, the soul of hospitality, quick to take offense, and quicker to forgive,—duellists as brave as Spartans, chivalric, proud of honor, their province, their blood and their families, they envied only one being in the world and that was he who could establish his claim to the possession of a strain from the veins of the dusky daughter of Powhatan—Pocahontas.

Could such people succeed as pioneers of the wilderness?

Into the snowy wastes of New England plunged the Pilgrims to blaze a path for civilization in the New World. They were perfect pioneers down to the minutest detail. Sturdy, grimly resolute, painfully honest, industrious, patient, moral and seeing God's hand in every affliction, they smothered their groans while writhing in the pangs of starvation and gasped in husky whispers: "He doeth all things well; praise to his name!" Such people could not fail in their work.

And yet of the first ten presidents, New England furnished only the two Adamses, while Virginia gave to the nation, Washington, Jefferson, Madison, Monroe and then tapered off with Tyler.

In the War for the Union, the ten most prominent leaders were Grant, Sherman, Sheridan, Thomas, Farragut, Porter, Lee, Stonewall Jackson, J. E. Johnston and Longstreet. Of these, four were the products of Virginia, while none came from New England, nor did she produce a real, military leader throughout the civil war, though she poured out treasure like water and sent as brave soldiers to the field as ever kept step to the drum beat, while in oratory, statesmanship and humanitarian achievement, her sons have been leaders from the foundation of the Republic.

Thomas Jefferson was born in Shadwell, Albemarle County, Va., April 2, 1743. His father was the owner of thirty slaves and of a wheat and tobacco farm of nearly two thousand acres. There were ten children, Thomas being the third. His father was considered the strongest man physically in the county, and the son grew to be like him in that respect, but the elder died while the younger was a boy.

Entering William and Mary College, Thomas was shy, but his ability quickly drew attention to him. He was an irrestrainable student, sometimes studying twelve and fourteen hours out of the twenty-four. He acquired the strength to stand this terrific strain by his exercise of body. His father warned his wife just before his death not to allow their son to neglect this necessity, but the warning was superfluous. The youth was a keen hunter, a fine horseman and as fond as Washington of out door sports.

He was seventeen years old when he entered college and was one of the "gawkiest" students. He was tall, growing fast, raw-boned, with prominent chin and cheek bones, big hands and feet, sandy-haired and freckled. His mind broadened and expanded fast under the tutelage of Dr. William Small, a Scotchman and the professor of mathematics, who made young Jefferson his companion in his walks, and showed an interest in the talented youth, which the latter gratefully remembered throughout life.

Jefferson was by choice a farmer and never lost interest in the management of his estate. One day, while a student at law, he wandered into the legislature and was thrilled by the glowing speech of Patrick Henry who replied to an interruption:

"If this be treason, make the most of it."

He became a lawyer in his twenty-fourth year, and was successful from the first, his practice soon growing to nearly five hundred cases annually, which yielded an income that would be a godsend to the majority of lawyers in these days.

Ere long, the mutterings of the coming Revolution drew Jefferson aside into the service of his country.

At the age of twenty-six (May 11, 1769), he took his seat in the House of Burgesses, of which Washington was a member. On the threshold of his public career, he made the resolution which was not once violated during his life, "never to engage, while in public office, in any kind of enterprise for the improvement of my fortune, nor to wear any other character than that of a farmer." Thus, during his career of nearly half a century, he was impartial in his consideration of questions of public interest.

His first important speech was in favor of the repeal of the law that compelled a master when he freed his slaves to send them out of the colony. The measure was overwhelmingly defeated, and its mover denounced as an enemy of his country.

It was about this time that Jefferson became interested in Mrs. Martha Wayles Skelton, a childless widow, beautiful and accomplished and a daughter of John Wayles, a prominent member of the Williamsburg bar. She was under twenty years of age, when she lost her first husband, rather tall, with luxuriant auburn hair and an exceedingly graceful manner.

She had many suitors, but showed no haste to lay aside her weeds. The aspirants indeed were so numerous that she might well hesitate whom to choose, and more than one was hopeful of winning the prize.

It so happened that one evening, two of the gentlemen called at the same time at her father's house. They were friends, and were about to pass from the hall into the drawing-room, when they paused at the sound of music. Some one was playing a violin with exquisite skill, accompanied by the harpsicord, and a lady and gentleman were singing.

There was no mistaking the violinist, for there was only one in the neighborhood capable of so artistic work, while Mrs.

Skelton had no superior as a player upon the harpsicord, the fashionable instrument of those days. Besides, it was easy to identify the rich, musical voice of Jefferson and the sweet tones of the young widow.

The gentlemen looked significantly at each other. Their feelings were the same.

"We are wasting our time," said one; "we may as well go home."

They quietly donned their hats and departed, leaving the ground to him who had manifestly already pre-empted it.

On New Year's day, 1772, Jefferson and Mrs. Skelton were married and no union was more happy. His affection was tender and romantic and they were devoted lovers throughout her life. Her health and wishes were his first consideration, and he resolved to accept no post or honor that would involve their separation, while she proved one of the truest wives with which any man was ever blessed of heaven. The death of his father-in-law doubled Jefferson's estate, a year after his marriage. His life as a gentleman farmer was an ideal one, and it is said that as a result of experimentation, Jefferson domesticated nearly every tree and shub, native and foreign, that was able to stand the Virginia winters.

Jefferson's commanding ability, however, speedily thrust him into the stirring incidents that opened the Revolution. In September, 1774, his "Draught of Instructions" for Virginia's delegation to the congress in Philadelphia was presented. The convention refused to adopt his radical views, but they were published in a pamphlet and copies were send to England, where Edmund Burke had it republished with emendations of his own.

Great Britain viewed the paper as the extreme of insolence and punished the author by adding his name to the list of proscriptions enrolled in a bill of attainder.

Jefferson was present as a member of the convention, which met in the parish church at Richmond, in March, 1775, to consider the course that Virginia should take in the impending crisis. It was at that meeting that Patrick Henry electrified his hearers with the thrilling words:

"Gentlemen may cry, 'Peace, peace!' but there is no peace! The war has actually begun! The next gale that sweeps from the North will bring to our ears the clash of resounding arms! Our brethren are already in the field. Why stand we here idle? What is it the gentlemen wish? What would they have? Is life so dear or peace so sweet as to be purchased at the price of chains and slavery? Forbid it, Almighty God! I know not what course others may take, but as for me, GIVE ME LIBERTY, Or GIVE ME DEATH!"

Within the following month occurred the battle of Lexington.

Washington, Jefferson and Patrick Henry were members of the committee appointed to arrange a plan for preparing Virginia to act her part in the struggle. When Washington, June, 20, 1775, received his commission as commander-in-chief of the American army, Jefferson succeeded to the vacancy thus created, and the next day took his seat in congress.

A few hours later came the news of the battle of Bunker Hill.

Jefferson was an influential member of the body from the first. John Adams said of him: "he was so prompt, frank, explicit and decisive upon committees that he soon seized upon every heart." Virginia promptly re-elected him and the part he took in draughting the Declaration of Independence is known to every school boy.

His associates on the committee were Franklin, John Adams, Roger Sherman and Robert R. Livingston. It was by their request that he prepared the document (see fac-simile, page 49,) done on the second floor of a small building, on the corner of Market and Seventh Streets. The house and the little desk, constructed by Jefferson himself, are carefully preserved.

The paper was warmly debated and revised in congress on the 2nd, 3rd and 4th of July, 1776. The weather was oppressively hot, and on the last day an exasperating but providential invasion of the hall by a swarm of flies hurried the signing of the document. Some days afterward, the committee of which Jefferson was a member provided as a motto of the new seal, that perfect legend,—E Pluribus Unum.

The facts connected with the adoption of the Declaration of Independence must always be of profound interest. The public are inclined to think that our Magna Charta was accepted and signed with unbounded enthusiasm and that scarcely any opposition to it appeared, but the contrary was the fact.

While Jefferson was the author of the instrument, John Adams, more than any one man or half a dozen men brought about its adoption. When the question was afterward asked him, whether every member of congress cordially approved it, he replied, "Majorities were constantly against it. For many days the majority depended on Mr. Hewes of North Carolina. While a member one day was reading documents to prove that public opinion was in favor of the measure, Mr. Hewes suddenly started upright, and lifting up both hands to heaven, as if in a trance, cried out:

'It is done, and I will abide by it.'

I would give more for a perfect painting of the terror and horror of the faces of the old majority at that moment than for the best piece of Raphael."

Jefferson has given a synopsis of the arguments for and against the adoption of the Declaration. It will be remembered that the hope of the colonies or new States, even after the war had continued for a considerable time, was not so much independence as to extort justice from Great Britain.

Had this been granted, the separation would have been deferred and when it came, as come it must, probably would have been peaceable. At the same time, there was a strenuous, aggressive minority who was insistent from the first for a complete severance of the ties binding us to the mother country.

The debate in congress showed that New York, New Jersey, Pennsylvania, Delaware, Maryland and South Carolina were not ready to take the irrevocable step, but it was evident that they were fast approaching that mood, and the wise leaders tarried in order to take them in their company.

In the vote of July 1, the Pennsylvania and South Carolina delegates still opposed, while those from New York did the same, contrary to their own convictions but in obedience to home instructions, which later were changed.

The signs of unanimity became unmistakable on the Second, and two days later, as every one knows. the adoption of the Declaration took place, though it was not until the Second of August that all the members, excepting John Dickinson had signed.

Five years passed before the Articles of Confederation were formally adopted by the states, by which time it had become clear that they must totally fail of their purpose, for each state decided for itself whether to respond to the demands of congress. The poison of nullification thus infused into the body politic at its birth bore baleful fruit in the years that followed.

On six separate occasions, there were overt acts on the part of the States.

The first occurred in 1798, when Virginia and Kentucky passed nullification resolutions.

The second was the attempt of New England in 1803 to form

a northern confederacy, comprising five New England States, and New York and New Jersey. The third was Aaron Burr's wild scheme in the Southwest.

The fourth, the resolution of the New England States to withold cooperation in the War of 1812.

The fifth, the nullification acts of South Carolina in 1832.

The sixth and last, the effort of eleven states to form the Southern Confederacy. This brought the burning issue to a head and settled the question for the ages to come.

It seems incredible in these times that the country submitted for a month to the intolerable Alien and Sedition acts. Should any congressman propose their reenactment to-day, he would be looked upon as a crank and be laughed out of court. They were enacted when Jefferson was Vice President and were the creation of the brilliant Alexander Hamilton, whose belief was in a monarchy rather than a republic.

The Sedition act made it a felony punishable with a fine of $5000 and five years imprisonment for persons to combine in order to impede the operation of any law of the United States, or to intimidate persons from taking Federal office, or to commit or advise a riot or insurrection or unlawful assembly.

It declared further that the writing or publishing of any scandalous, malicious or false statement against the president or either house of congress should be punishable by a fine of $2000 and imprisonment for two years.

It will be noted that this law precluded all free discussion of an act of congress, or the conduct of the president.

In other words, it was meant to be the death blow to freedom of speech.

But bad as it was, the Alien act, which congress passed at the same session, 1798, was ten fold worse.

There had been much unrest caused by the intermeddling of foreigners in the States, and it was now decided that the president might drive out of the country any alien he chose thus to banish, and to do it without assigning any reason therefor. It was not necessary even to sue or to bring charges; if an alien receiving such notice from the president refused to obey, he could be imprisoned for three years.

President Adams afterward declared that he did not approve of this stern measure which was the work of Hamilton, and boasted that it was not enforced by him in a single instance.

Nevertheless, the Sedition act was enforced to a farcical degree.

When President Adams was passing through Newark, N. J., he was saluted by the firing of cannon. One of the cannoneers, who was strongly opposed to him, expressed the wish that he might be struck by some of the wadding. For this remark, he was arrested and compelled to pay a fine of one hundred dollars.

Editor Frothingham printed his belief that Hamilton wished to buy the Aurora for the purpose of suppressing it. For expressing that opinion he was fined and imprisoned. Thomas Cooper made the remark that in 1797 President Adams was "hardly in the infancy of political mistakes," and these mild words cost him $400 and kept him in prison for six months.

It is hard to believe that the following proceedings took place within the present hundred years in the United States of America, and yet they did.

In the case against Callender, Judge Chase denounced the accused to the jurors and forbade the marshals to place any one not a Federalist on the jury. The lawyers who defended Callender were threatened with corporal punishment.

In Otsego, N. Y., Judge Peck obtained signers to a petition for the repeal of the obnoxious acts. For such action he was indicted and taken to New York city for trial.

That was the sacred right of petition with a vengeance.

Matthew Lyon, while canvassing his district in Vermont for re-election to congress, charged the president in one of his speeches with "unbounded thirst for ridiculous pomp, foolish adulation and a selfish avarice," certainly mild expressions compared with what are heard in these times, but because of their utterance, Mr. Lyon spent four months in jail and paid a fine of $1000.

When he had served out his term and been re-elected, a strong effort was made to prevent his taking his seat. It failed and in 1840, his fine was returned to him with interest.

It can well be understood that the passage and enforcement of such iniquitous measures caused alarm and indignation throughout the country.

Edward Livingston declared that they would "disgrace Gothic barbarism." Jefferson's soul was stirred with the profoundest indignation. Under his inspiration, the Virginia assembly adopted resolutions calling on the state to nullify within its limits the enforcement of the Sedition act. The Alien and Sedition laws were declared unconstitutional, and the sister States were invited to unite in resisting them, "in order to maintain unimpaired the authorities, rights and liberties reserved to the States respectively or to the people."

These views were not only those of Jefferson, but of Patrick Henry, George Mason and nearly all leading Virginians.

Kentucky, the child of her loins, seconded the action of Virginia, urged thereto by Jefferson who moulded her resolutions.

The revolt against the measures was so widespread that the Alien act was repealed in 1800, and the Sedition act in the following year.

Having been essentially Federal measures, they were buried in the same grave with the Federal party.

Having rendered these invaluable services, Jefferson resigned his seat in congress, on account of the illness of his wife and the urgent need of his presence at home. Moreover, he had been elected a member of the legislature of his State and was anxious to purge its statute books of a number of objectionable laws.

He had hardly entered upon the work, when he was notified of his appointment as a joint commissioner with Franklin and Deane as representatives of the United States in France. After reflection, he declined the appointment, believing his duty at home was more important. That such was the fact was proven by his success in securing the repeal of the system of entail, thus allowing all property in the State to be held in fee simple, and by the abolishment of the connection between church and state. The latter required years in order to effect complete success, but it was reached at last.

How forceful were many of the expressions he employed during that contest, such as: "Compulsion makes hypocrites, not converts;" "Truth stands by itself; error alone needs the support of government."

Jefferson's committee abolished the frightful penalties of the ancient code; he set on foot the movement for the improvement of public education; he drew the bill for the establishment of courts of law in the State, and prescribing their methods and powers; he destroyed the principle of primogeniture, and brought about the removal of the capital from Williamsburg to Richmond.

Jefferson succeeded Patrick Henry as Governor of the State, at the opening of the year 1779. The two years were marked by incessant trial and the severest labor, for the war had reached Virginia soil and the State was desolated.

More than once the legislature was obliged to flee before the enemy; Gates was crushed at Camden; Arnold the traitor scourged Richmond with his raiders; Monticello itself was captured by cavalry, and Jefferson escaped only by a hair's breadth. His estate was trampled over, his horses stolen, his barns burned, his crops destroyed and many of his slaves run off.

He declined a third election,and in the autumn of 1782, to his inconsolable sorrow, his wife died, leaving three daughters, the youngest a babe.

In the following November, he took his seat in congress at Annapolis, and during that session he proposed and caused the adoption of our present system of decimal currency.

In May, 1784, he was again elected plenipotentiary to France to assist Franklin and Adams in negotiating commercial treaties with foreign nations. He arrived in Paris in July, and in May, succeeding, became sole plenipotentiary to the king of France for three years from March 1O, 1785.

Jefferson's residence in France produced a profound impression upon him and had much to do in crystallizing his ideas of the true form of government.

That country was groveling under the heel of one of the most hideous systems that the baseness of man ever conceived. Who has not read of the nobleman who, when his coachman ran over a child and crushed out its life, was only concerned lest its blood should soil his carriage, or of the poor peasants who were compelled to beat the bogs all night long, to prevent the frogs from croaking and thereby disturbing the slumber of their lordly masters? The condition of no people could be more horrible, than that of the lower classes in France previous to the uprising, with its excesses that horrified the world.

Jefferson enjoyed the music, the art and the culture of the gay capital, but could never shake off the oppression caused by the misery of the people.

"They are ground to powder," he said, "by the vices of the form of government which is one of wolves over sheep, or kites over pigeons."

He took many journeys through the country and made it a practice to enter the houses of the peasants and talk with them upon their affairs and manner of living. He often did this, using his eyes at the same time with the utmost assiduity. All that he learned deepened the sad impression he had formed, and he saw with unerring prevision the appalling retribution that was at hand.

But Jefferson was not the officer to forget or neglect his duties to his own government, during the five years spent in France.

Algiers, one of the pestilent Barbary States, held a number of American captives which she refused to release except upon the payment of a large ransom. It had been the custom for years for the powerful Christian nations to pay those savages to let their ships alone, because it was cheaper to do so than to maintain a fleet to fight them. Jefferson strove to bring about a union of several nations with his own, for the purpose of pounding some sense into the heads of the barbarians and compelling them to behave themselves.

One reason why he did not succeed was because our own country had no navy with which to perform her part in the compact.

France, with that idiotic blindness which ruled her in those fearful days, maintained a protective system which prevented America from sending cheap food to starving people, nor was Jefferson able to effect more than a slight change in the pernicious law. One thing done by him made him popular with the masses. His "Notes on Virginia" was published both in French and English. Like everything that emanated from his master hand, it was well conceived and full of information. In addition, it glowed with republican sentiment and delighted the people. He was in Paris when his State legislature enacted the act for which he had so strenuously worked, establishing the freedom of religion. He had numerous copies of it printed in French and distributed. It struck another popular chord and received the ardent praise of the advanced Liberals.

Jefferson was too deeply interested in educational work to forget it among any surroundings. All new discoveries, inventions and scientific books were brought to the knowledge of the colleges in the United States, and he collected a vast quantity of seeds, roots and nuts for transplanting in American soil.

It need hardly be said that his loved Monticello was not forgotten, and, as stated elswhere, he grew about everything of that nature that would stand the rigor of the Virginia winters. No office or honor could take away Jefferson's pride as a cultivator of the soil.

Returning to Virginia on leave of absence, in the autumn of 1789, he was welcomed with official honors and the cordial respect of his fellow citizens. On the same day he learned of his appointment by Washington as his Secretary of State.

He would have preferred to return to his former post, but yielded to the wishes of the first president, and, arriving in New York in March, 1790, entered at once upon the duties of his office.

In the cabinet Jefferson immediately collided with the brilliant Alexander Hamilton, Secretary of the Treasury.

The two could no more agree than oil and water.

Jefferson was an intense republican-democrat, and was shocked and disgusted to find himself in an atmosphere of distrust of a republican system of government, with an unmistakable leaning toward monarchical methods. This feeling prevailed not only in society, but showed itself among the political leaders.

Jefferson's political creed may be summed up in his own words:

"The will of the majority is the natural law of every society and the only sure guardian of the rights of man; though this may err, yet its errors are honest, solitary and short-lived. We are safe with that, even in its deviations, for it soon returns again to the right way."

Hamilton believed in a strong, centralized government, and on nearly every measure that came before the cabinet, these intellectual giants wrangled. Their quarrels were so sharp that Washington was often distressed. He respected both too deeply to be willing to lose either, but it required all his tact and mastering influence to hold them in check. Each found the other so intolerable, that he wished to resign that he might be freed from meeting him.

Hamilton abhorred the French revolution, with its terrifying excesses, and Jefferson declared that no horror equalled that of France's old system of government.

Finally Jefferson could stand it no longer and withdrew from the cabinet January 1, 1794.

An equally potent cause for his resignation was the meagreness of his salary of $3500. It was wholly insufficient and his estate was going to ruin. He yearned to return to his beloved pursuit, that of a farmer.

The request by Washington to act as special envoy to Spain did not tempt him, but he allowed his name to be put forward as a candidate for the presidency in 1796. John Adams received 71 votes and Jefferson 68, which in accordance with the law at that time made him vice-president.

President Adams ignored him in all political matters, and Jefferson found the chair of presiding officer of the senate congenial. He presided with dignity and great acceptability, and his "Manual of Parliamentary Practice" is still the accepted authority in nearly all of our deliberative bodies.

The presidential election of 1800 will always retain its place among the most memorable in our history.

The Federalists had controlled the national government for twelve years, or ever since its organization, and they were determined to prevent the elevation of Jefferson, the founder of the new Republican party. The Federal nominees were John Adams for president and Charles Cotesworth Pinckney for vice-president, while the Republican vote was divided between Jefferson and Aaron Burr.

A favorite warning on the part of those who see their ideas threatened with overthrow is that our country is "trembling on the verge of revolution." How many times in the past twenty-five, ten and five years have ranting men and women proclaimed from the housetops that we were "on the verge of revolution?" According to these wild pessimists the revolution is always at hand, but somehow or other it fails to arrive. The probabilities are that it has been permanently side-tracked.

During the campaign of 1800, Hamilton sounded the trumpet of alarm, when he declared in response to a toast:

"If Mr. Pinckney is not elected, a revolution will be the consequence, and within four years I will lose my head or be the leader of a triumphant army."

The Federalist clergy joined in denouncing Jefferson on the ground that he was an atheist. The Federalists said what they chose, but when the Republicans grew too careless they were fined and imprisoned under the Sedition law.

The exciting canvas established one fact: there was no man in the United States so devotedly loved and so fiercely hated as Thomas Jefferson. New York had twelve electoral votes, and because of the Alien and Sedition laws she witheld them from Adams and cast them upon the Republican side.

It may not be generally known that it was because of this fact that New York gained its name of the "Empire State."

The presidential vote was: Jefferson, 73; Burr, 73; John Adams, 65; C. C. Pinckney, 64; Jay, 1. There being a tie between the leading candidates, the election was thrown into the House of Representatives, which assembled on the 11th of February, 1801, to make choice between Burr and Jefferson.

It is to the credit of Hamilton that, knowing the debased character of Burr, he used his utmost influence against him.

A great snow storm descended upon the little town of Washington and the excitement became intense. On the first ballot, eight States voted for Jefferson and six for Burr, while Maryland and Vermont were equally divided. All the Federalists voted for Burr with the single exception of Huger of South Carolina, not because of any love for Burr, but because he did not hate him as much as he did Jefferson.

Mr. Nicholson of Maryland was too ill to leave his bed. Without his vote, his State would have been given to Burr, but with it, the result in Maryland would be a tie.

It was a time when illness had to give way to the stern necessity of the case, and the invalid was wrapped up and brought on his bed through the driving snow storm and placed in one of the committee rooms of the house, with his wife at his side, administering medicines and stimulants night and day. On each vote the ballot box was brought to the bed side and his feeble hand deposited the powerful bit of paper.

Day after day, the balloting went on until thirty-five ballots had been cast.

By that time, it was clear that no break could be made in the Jefferson columns and it was impossible to elect Burr. When the thirty-sixth ballot was cast, the Federalists of Maryland, Delaware and South Carolina threw blanks and the Federalists of Vermont stayed away, leaving their Republican brothers to vote those States for Jefferson. By this slender chance did the republic escape a calamity, and secure the election of Jefferson for president with Burr for vice-president.

The inauguration of the third president was made a national holiday throughout the country. The church bells were rung, the military paraded, joyous orations were delivered,and many of the newspapers printed in full the Declaration of Independence.

The closeness of the election resulted in a change in the electoral law by which the president and vice-president must of necessity belong to the same political party.

Jefferson had every reason to feel proud of his triumph, but one of the finest traits of his character was his magnanimity.

The irascible Adams made an exhibition of himself on the 4th of March, when in a fit of rage, he rose before day-light and set out in his coach for Massachusetts, refusing to wait and take part in the inauguration of his successor. With the mellowness of growing years, he realized the silliness of the act, and he and Jefferson became fully reconciled and kept up an affectionate correspondence to the end of their lives.

Jefferson did all he could to soothe the violent party feeling that had been roused during the election. This spirit ran like a golden thread through his first excellently conceived inaugural. He reminded his fellow citizens that while they differed in opinion, there was no difference in principle, and put forth the following happy thought:

"We are all Republicans, we are all Federalists. If there be any among us, who would wish to dissolve this Union or to change its republican form, let them stand undisturbed as monuments of the safety with which error of opinion may be tolerated where reason is left free to combat it."

There can be little doubt that he had Hamilton in mind when he answered, as follows, in his own forceful way the radical views of that gifted statesman.

"Some honest men fear that a republican government cannot be strong, that this government is not strong enough. I believe this, on the contrary, is the strongest government on earth. I believe it is the only one where every man, at the call of the laws, would fly to the standard of the law, and would meet invasions of the public order as his own personal concern."

It was characteristic of Jefferson's nobility that one of his first efforts was to undo, so far as he could, the mischief effected by the detested Sedition law. Every man who was in durance because of its operation was pardoned, and he looked upon the law as "a nullity as obsolete and palpable, as if congress had ordered us to fall down and worship a golden image."

He addressed friendly and affectionate letters to Kosciusko and others, and invited them to be his guests at the White House. Samuel Adams of Massachusetts had been shamefully abused during the canvas, but he felt fully compensated by the touching letter from the president. Thomas Paine was suffering almost the pangs of starvation in Paris, and Jefferson paid his passage home. Everywhere that it was possible for Jefferson to extend the helping hand he did so with a delicacy and a tact, that won him multitudes of friends and stamped him as one of nature's noblemen.

The new president selected an able cabinet, consisting of James

Madison, Secretary of State; Albert Gallatin, Secretary of the Treasury; Henry Dearborn, Secretary of War; Robert Smith, Secretary of the Navy; Gideon Granger, Postmaster-general; Levi Lincoln, Attorney General. This household proved a veritable "happy family," all working together in harmony throughout the two terms, and Jefferson declared that if he had his work to do over again, he would select the same advisers without exception.

Although the policy,"to the victors belong the spoils," had not been formulated at that time, its spirit quickened the body politic. Jefferson's supporters expected him to turn out a part at least of the Federalists, who held nearly all the offices, but he refused, on the principle that a competent and honest office holder should not be removed because of his political opinions. When he, therefore, made a removal, it was as a rule, for other and sufficient reasons.

But he did not hesitate to show his dislike of the ceremony that prevailed around him. He stopped the weekly levee at the White House, and the system of precedence in force at the present time; also the appointment of fast and thanksgiving days. He dressed with severe simplicity and would not permit any attention to be paid him as president which would be refused him as a private citizen. In some respects, it must be conceded that this remarkable man carried his views to an extreme point.

The story, however, that he rode his horse alone to the capitol, and, tying him to the fence, entered the building, unattended, lacks confirmation.

Jefferson was re-elected in 1804, by a vote of 162 to 14 for Pinckney, who carried only two States out of the seventeen.

The administrations of Jefferson were marked not only by many important national events, but were accompanied by great changes in the people themselves. Before and for some years after the Revolution, the majority were content to leave the task of thinking, speaking and acting to the representatives, first of the crown and then to their influential neighbors. The property qualification abridged the right to vote, but the active, hustling nature of the Americans now began to assert itself. The universal custom of wearing wigs and queues was given up and men cut their own hair short and insisted that every free man should have the right to vote.

Jefferson was the founder and head of the new order of things, and of the republican party, soon to take the name of democratic, which controlled all the country with the exception of New England.

Our commerce increased enormously, for the leading nations of Europe were warring with one another; money came in fast and most of the national debt was paid.

Louisiana with an area exceeding all the rest of the United States, was bought from France in 1803, for $15,000,000, and from the territory were afterward carved the states of Louisiana, Arkansas, Missouri, Iowa, Kansas, Nebraska, the Dakotas, Montana, Oklahoma, the Indian Territory and most of the states of Wisconsin, Minnesota, Colorado and Wyoming.

The upper Missouri River and the Columbia River country to the Pacific Ocean were explored in 1804-6, by Lewis and Clarke, the first party of white men to cross the continent north of Mexico. Ohio was admitted to the Union in 1802. Fulton's steamboat, the Clermont made her maiden trip from New York to Albany in 1807. The first boatload of anthracite coal was shipped to Philadelphia, and it was a long time before the people knew what to do with it.

The Tripolitan Pirates were snuffed out (1801-1805). The blight of the Embargo Act settled upon our commerce in 1807, in which year the opening gun of the War of 1812 was fired when the Leopard outraged the Chesapeake.

The Embargo Act was a grievous mistake of Jefferson, though its purpose was commendable. Under the plea of securing our ships against capture, its real object was to deprive England and France of the commodities which could be secured only in the United States. This measure might have been endurable for an agricultural people, but it could not be borne by a commercial and manufacturing one, like New England, whose goods must find their market abroad. Under the Embargo Act, the New England ships were rotting and crumbling to pieces at her wharves. It was not long before she became restless. The measure was first endorsed by the Massachusetts legislature, but the next session denounced it.

Early in 1809, congress passed an act allowing the use of the army and navy to enforce the embargo and make seizures.

The Boston papers printed the act in mourning and, meetings were called to memorialize the legislature. That body took strong ground, justifying the course of Great Britain, demanding of congress that it should repeal the embargo and declare war against France. Moreover, the enforcement act was declared "not legally binding," and resistance to it was urged.

This was as clear a case of nullification as that of South Carolina in 1832.

Connecticut was as hot-headed as Massachusetts.

John Quincy Adams has stated that at that time the "Essex Junto" agreed upon a New England convention to consider the expediency of secession. Adams denounced the plotters so violently that the Massachusetts legislature censured him by vote, upon which he resigned his seat in the United States senate.

The Embargo Act was passed by congress, December 22, 1807, at the instance of Jefferson, and repealed February 28, 1809, being succeeded by the Non-Intercourse Act, which forbade French and British vessels to enter American ports. It was mainly due to Jefferson's consummate tact that war with Great Britain was averted after the Leopard and Chesapeake affair, and he always maintained that had his views been honestly carried out by the entire nation, we should have obtained all we afterward fought for, without the firing of a hostile gun.

When on March 4, 1809, Jefferson withdrew forever from public life, he was in danger of being arrested in Washington for debt. He was in great distress, but a Richmond bank helped him for a time with a loan. He returned to Monticello, where he lived with his only surviving daughter Martha, her husband and numerous children, and with the children of his daughter Maria, who had died in 1804.

He devoted hard labor and many years to the perfection of the common school system in Virginia, and was so pleased with his establishment of the college at Charlottesville, out of which grew the University of Virginia, that he had engraved on his tombstone, "Father of the University of Virginia," and was prouder of the fact than of being the author of the Declaration of Independence.

Meanwhile, his lavish hospitality carried him lower and lower into poverty. There was a continual procession of curious visitors to Monticello, and old women poked their umbrellas through the window panes to get a better view of the grand old man. Congress in 1814, paid him $23,000 for his library which was not half its value. Some time afterward a neighbor obtained his name as security on a note for $20,000 and left him to pay it all.

In the last year of his life, when almost on the verge of want, $16,500 was sent to him as a present from friends in New York, Philadelphia and Baltimore, more than one-half being raised by Mayor Hone of New York. Jefferson was moved to tears, and in expressing his gratitude said, he was thankful that not a penny had been wrung from taxpayers.

In the serene sunset of life, the "Sage of Monticello" peacefully passed away on the afternoon of July 4, 1826, and a few hours later, John Adams, at his home in Quincy, Mass., breathed his last. A reverent hush fell upon the country, at the thought of these two great men, one the author of the Declaration of Independence and the other the man who brought about its adoption, dying on the fiftieth anniversary of its signing, and many saw a sacred significance in the fact.

Horace Greeley in referring to the co-incidence, said there was as much probability of a bushel of type flung into the street arranging themselves so as to print the Declaration of Independence, as there was of Jefferson and Adams expiring on the fiftieth anniversary of the adoption of that instrument; and yet one alternative of the contingency happened and the other never can happen.

Jefferson's liberal views have caused him to be charged with infidelity.

He profoundly respected the moral character of Christ, but did not believe in divine redemption through Christ's work. His dearest aim was to bring down the aristocracy and elevate the masses.

He regarded slavery as a great moral and political evil, and in referring to it said: "I tremble for my country when I remember that God is just."

No more humane slave owner ever lived, and his servants regarded him with almost idolatrous affection, while his love of justice, his hospitality, his fairness to all and his winning personality disarmed enmity and gave him many of his truest and warmest friends from among his political opponents.

A peculiar fact connected with Jefferson is the difference among his portraits. This is due to the varying periods at which they were made. As we have stated, he was raw-boned, freckled and ungainly in his youth, but showed a marked improvement in middle life. When he became old, many esteemed him good looking, though it can hardly be claimed that he was handsome.

When Jefferson was eighty years old, Daniel Webster wrote the following description of the venerable "Sage of Monticello:"

"Never in my life did I see his countenance distorted by a single bad passion or unworthy feeling. I have seen the expression of suffering, bodily and mental, of grief, pain, sadness, disagreeable surprise and displeasure, but never of anger, impatience, peevishness, discontent, to say nothing of worse or more ignoble emotions. To the contrary, it was impossible to look on his face without being struck with the benevolent, intelligent, cheerful and placid expression. It was at once intellectual, good, kind and pleasant, whilst his tall, spare figure spoke of health, activity and that helpfulness, that power and will, 'never to trouble another for what he could do himself,' which marked his character."

This sketch may well be closed with Jefferson's own words regarding life and happiness.

"Perfect happiness, I believe, was never intended by the Deity to be the lot of one of his creatures in this world; but that He has very much put it in our power the nearness of our approach to it, is what I have steadfastly believed.

The most fortunate of us, in our journey through life, frequently meet with calamities and misfortunes, which may greatly afflict us; and to fortify our minds against the attacks of these calamities and misfortunes should be one of the principal studies and endeavors of our lives.

The only method of doing this is to assume a perfect resignation to the Divine will, to consider that whatever does happen must happen, and that by our uneasiness we cannot prevent the blow before it does fall, but we may add to its force after it has fallen.

These considerations, and others such as these, may enable us in some measure to surmount the difficulties thrown in our way, to bear up with a tolerable degree of patience under this burden of life, and to proceed with a pious and unshaken resignation till we arrive at our journey's end, when we may deliver up our trust into the hands of Him who gave it, and receive such reward as to Him shall seem proportionate to our merits."

THOMAS JEFFERSON (1743-1826)
BY G. MERCER ADAM

JEFFERSON, when he penned the famous Declaration of Independence, which broke all hope of reconciliation with the motherland and showed England what the deeply-wronged Colonies of the New World unitedly desired and would in the last resort fight for, had then just passed his thirty-third birthday. Who was the man, and what were his upbringings and status in the then young community, that inspired the writing of this great historic document— a document that on its adoption gave these United States an ever-memorable national birthday, and seven years later, by the Peace of Versailles, wrung from Britain recognition of the independence of the country and ushered it into the great sisterhood of Nations? To his contemporaries and a later political age, Jefferson, in spite of his culture and the aristocratic strain in his blood, is known as the advocate of popular sovereignty and the champion of democracy in matters governmental, as United States minister to France between the years 1784-89, as Secretary of State under Washington, and as U. S. President from 1801 to 1809. By education and bent of mind, he was, however, an idealist in politics, a thinker and writer, rather than a debater and speaker, and one who in his private letters, State papers, and public documents did much to throw light, in his era, on the origin and development of American political thought. A man of fine education and of noble, elevated character, he earned distinction among his fellows, and though opposed politically by many prominent statesmen of the day, who, like Washington, Hamilton, and Adams, were in favor of a strong centralized government, while Jefferson, in the interests of the masses, feared encroachments on State and individual liberty, he was nevertheless paid the respect, consideration, and regard of his generation, as his services have earned the gratitude and his memory the endearing commendation of posterity.

The illustrous statesman was born April 13, 1743, at "Shadwell," his father's home in the hill country of central Virginia, about 150 miles from Williamsburg, once the capital of the State, and the seat of William and Mary college, where Jefferson received his higher education. His father, Peter Jefferson, was a planter, owning an estate of about 2,000 acres, cultivated, as was usual in Virginia, by slave labor. His mother was a Miss Randolph, and well connected; to her the future President owed his aristocratic blood and refined tastes, and with good looks a fine, manly presence. By her, Thomas, who was the third of nine children, was in his childhood's days gently nurtured, though himself fond of outdoor life and invigorating physical exercise. His father died when his son was but fourteen, and to him he bequeathed the Roanoke River estate, afterwards rebuilt and christened "Monticello." His studies at the time were pursued under a fairly good classical scholar; and on passing to college he there made diligent use of his time in the study of history, literature, the sciences, and mathematics.

When he left college Jefferson took up the study of law under the direction of George Wythe, afterwards Chancellor, then a rising professional man of high attainments, to whom the youth seems to have been greatly indebted as mentor and warm, abiding friend. He was also fortunate in the acquaintance he was able to make among many of the best people of Virginia, including some historic names, such as Patrick Henry, Edmund Randolph, and Francis Fauquier, the lieutenant-governor of the province, a gentleman with strong French proclivities, and a devoted student of the destructive writings of Voltaire, Rousseau, and Diderot, that had much to do in bringing on the French Revolution. By his father's death, he acquired a modest income, besides his little estate, and the former he added to by his legal practice when, in 1767, he obtained his diploma as a lawyer. In 1769, he became a member of the House of Burgesses along with Washington and other prominent Virginians, and with the exception of brief intervals he served with distinction until the outbreak of the Revolution. In 1772, he married a young widow in good circumstances, and this enabled him to add alike to his income and to his patrimony. About the time of the meeting of the Colonial Convention, called in 1775, to choose delegates for the Continental Congress at Philadelphia, at which Patrick Henry was present, the youthful Jefferson, now known as an able political writer, wrote his "Summary View of the Rights of British America"—a trenchant protest against English taxation of the Colonies, which had considerable influence in creating public feeling favorable to American Independence.

The effect of this notable utterance was, later on, vastly increased by the draft he prepared of the Declaration of Independence, the latter immortal document being somewhat of a transcript of views set forth by Jefferson in his former paper, as well as of ideas expressed by the English philosopher, John Locke, in his "Theory of Government," and by Rosseau, in his "Discourse on the Origin of Inequality Among Men;" though the circumstances of the Colonies at this time were of course different; while to England and the European nations the Declaration was a startling revelation of the attitude now assumed by the great leaders of the movement for separation as well as for freedom and independence. In the passing of this great national charter John Adams, as all know, was of much service to Jefferson in the debate over it in committee, as well as in the subsequent ratification of it by the House. Franklin was also of assistance in its revision in draft form; and most happy was the result, not only in the ultimate passing of the great historic document, but in its affirmation of the intelligent stand taken by the Colonies against England and her monarch, and in its pointed definition of the theory of democratic government on which the new fabric of popular rule in the New World was founded and raised.

In the autumn of 1776, Jefferson resigned his seat in Congress, or rather declined re-election to the Third Continental Congress, and retired for a time to his Virginia home. He also, at this period, declined appointment to France on the mission on which Franklin had set out; nevertheless, we presently find him a member of the legislature of his own State, taking part in passing measures in which he was particularly interested. Many of these measures are indicative of the breadth of mind and large, tolerant views for which Jefferson was noted, viz.: the repeal in Virginia of the laws of entail; the abolition of primogeniture and the substitution of equal partition of inheritance; the affirmation of the rights of conscience and the relief of the people from taxation for the support of a religion not their own; and the introduction of a general system of education, so that the people, as the author of these beneficent acts himself expressed it, "would be qualified to understand their rights, to maintain them, and to exercise with intelligence their parts in self-government." Other measures included the abolition of capital punishment, save for murder and treason, and an embargo placed on the importation of slaves, though Jefferson failed in his larger design of freeing all slaves, as he desired, hoping that this would be done throughout the entire country, while also beneficently extending to them white aid and protection.

In 1779, Jefferson succeeded Patrick Henry in the governorship of Virginia. This was the period when the English were prosecuting their campaigns in the South, checked by General Nathaniel Greene—when South Carolina was being overrun by Cornwallis, and Virginia itself was invaded by expeditions from New York under Philips and Arnold. As Jefferson had no military abilities, indeed, was a recluse rather than a man of action, the administration of his native Province, while able and efficient, was lacking in the notable incident which the then crisis of affairs would naturally call forth. Even his own Virginia homestead was at this time raided by the English cavalry officer, Colonel Tarleton, and much of his property was either desolated or stolen. This occasioned bitter resentment against the English in Jefferson's mind; while the serious illness and early death of his loved wife, which occurred just then, led him to surrender office and return for a time to the seclusion of his home.

Meanwhile, thrice was the offer made to the fast-budding statesman to proceed to France as ambassador; and only on the post being pressed upon him for the fourth time did he accept its duties and responsibilities and set out, accompanied by a daughter whom he wished to have educated abroad, for Paris in the summer of 1784.

In the post now vacated by Franklin, Jefferson remained for five years, until the meeting of the French Estates-General and the outbreak of the Revolution against absolute monarchy and the theory of the State in France upon which it rested. With French society, Jefferson, even more than his predecessor, was greatly enamored, and was on intimate terms with the savants of the era, including those who by their writings had precipitated the French Revolution, with all its excesses and horrors. The latter, it is true, filled Jefferson with dismay on his return to America, though dear to him were the principles which the apostles of revolution advocated and the wellbeing of the people, in spite of the anarchy that ensued. What diplomatic business was called for during his holding the post of minister, Jefferson efficiently conducted, and with the courtesy as well as sagacity which marked all his relations as a publicist and man of the world. Unlike John Adams, who with Franklin had been his predecessor as American envoy to France, he was on good terms with the French minister, Count Vergennes; while he shut his eyes, which Adams could not do, to the lack of disinterestedness in French friendliness toward the Colonies and remembered only the practical and timely service the nation had rendered to his country. Jefferson added to his services at this era by his efforts to suppress piracy in the Mediterranean, on the part of corsairs belonging to the Barbary States, which he further checked, later on, by the bombardment of Tripoli and the punishment administered to Algiers during the Tripolitan war (1801-05), for her piratical attacks on neutral commerce.

After traveling considerably through Europe and informing himself as to the character and condition of the people in the several countries visited, Jefferson returned to America just at the time when Washington was elected to the Presidency. In his absence, the Federal Convention had met at Philadelphia, the Constitution of the United States had been adopted and ratified, and the government had been organized with its executive departments, then limited to five, viz.: The State Department, the Treasury, the War Department, the Department of Justice, and the Post-office. The Judiciary had also been organized and the Supreme Court founded. With these organizations of the machinery of government came presently the founding of parties, especially the rise of the Republican or Democratic party, as it was subsequently called, in opposition to the Federalist party, then led by Hamilton, Jay, and Morris. At this juncture, on the return of Jefferson from the French mission, and after a visit to his home in Virginia, Washington offered him the post of Secretary of State, which he accepted, and entered upon the duties of that office in New York in March, 1791. His chief colleague in the Cabinet, soon now to become his political opponent, was Alexander Hamilton, who had charge of the finances, as head of the Treasury department. Between these two men, as chiefs of the principal departments of government, President Washington had an anxious time of it in keeping the peace, for each was insistently arrayed against the other, not only in their respective attitudes toward England and in the policy of the administration in the then threatening war with France, but also as to the powers the National Government should be entrusted with in relation to the legislatures of the separate states. What Jefferson specially feared, with his firmly held views as to the independence of public opinion, and especially his hatred of monarchy and all its ways, was that the conservative and aristocratic influences of the envirnoment [sic] of New York, hardly as yet escaped from the era of royal and Tory dominion and submission to the English Crown, might fashion the newly federated nation upon English models and give it a complexion far removed, socially as well as politically, from Republican simplicity, coupled with a disposition to aggress upon and dictate to the individual states of the Union, to their nullification and practical effacement.

For this apparent tendency, Jefferson specially blamed Hamilton, since his tastes as well as his sympathies were known to be aristocratic, as indeed were Washington's, in his fondness for courtly dignity and the trappings and ceremonies of high office. But his antagonism to Hamilton was specially called forth by the latter's creation of a National Bank, with its tendency to aggrandize power and coerce or control votes at the expense of the separate States. He further was opposed to the great financier and aristocrat for his leanings toward England and against France, in the war that had then broken out between these nations, and for his sharp criticism of the draft of the message to Congress on the relations of France and England, which Jefferson had penned, and which was afterwards to influence Washington in issuing the Neutrality Proclamation of 1793. In this attitude toward Hamilton and the administration, of which both men were members, Jefferson was neither selfish nor scheming, but, on the contrary, was discreet and patriotic, as well as just and high-minded. "What he desired supremely," as has been well stated by a writer, "was the triumph of democratic principles, since he saw in this triumph the welfare of the country—the interests of the many against the ascendancy of the few—the real reign of the people, instead of the reign of an aristocracy of money or birth." In this opposition to his chief and able colleague, and feeling strongly on the matters which constantly brought him into collision with the centralizing designs of the President and the preponderating influence in the Cabinet hostile to his views, Jefferson resigned his post in December, 1793, and retired for a time to his estate at Monticello.

Jefferson always relished the period of his brief retirements to his Virginia home, where he could enjoy his library, entertain his friends, and overlook his estates. There, too, he took a lively interest in popular and higher education, varied by outlooks on the National situation, not always pleasing to him, as in the case of Jay's treaty with England (1794-95), which shortly afterwards proved fatal to that statesman's candidature for the Presidential office. Meanwhile, the contentions and rivalries of the political parties grew apace; and in 1797, just before the retirement of Washington at the close of his second administration, the struggle between Democrats and Federalists became focussed on the prize of the Presidency—the "Father of his Country" having declined to stand for a third term. The candidates, we need hardly say, were John Adams, who had been Vice President in Washington's administration, and Thomas Jefferson, the former being the standard-bearer of the Federalists, and the latter the candidate of the anti-Federal Republicans. The contest ended by Adams securing the Presidency by three votes (71 to 68) over Jefferson, who thus, acording to the usage of the time, became Vice-President.

The Adams' Administration, though checkered by divided counsels and by the machinations of party, was on the whole beneficial to the country. It had, however, to face new complications with France, then under the Directory. These complications arose, in part, from soreness over the passing of the Jay treaty with England, and in part because America could not be bled for money through its envoys, at the bidding of unscrupulous members of the Directory. The situation was for a time so grave as to incite to war preparations in the United States, and to threatened naval demonstrations against France. Nor were matters improved by the enforcement of the Alien and Sedition Acts (1798), directed against those deemed dangerous to the peace and safety of the country, or who, like the more violent members of the Press, published libels on the Government. The storm which these obnoxious Acts evoked led to their speedy repeal, though not before Jefferson and Madison had denounced them as fetters on the freedom of public speech and infringements of the rights of the people. They were moreover resented as not being in harmony with the Constitution, as a compact to which the individual States of the Union were parties, and which Jefferson especially deemed to be in jeopardy from Federalist legislation.

The result of these agitations of the period, and of breaches, which had now come about, between the Adams and Hamilton wings of the Federalist party, showed itself in the Presidential campaign of 1800. Washington, by this time, had passed from earthly scenes, and the coming nineteenth century was to bring such changes and developments in the young nation as few then foresaw or even dreamed of. At this era, when the Adams Administration was about to close, Jefferson, in spite of his known liberal, democratic views, was one of the most popular of political leaders, save with the Federalists, now dwindling in numbers and influence. He it was who was put forward on the Republican side for the Presidency, while Adams, still favored by the Federalists and himself desiring a second term of office, became the Federalist candidate. Associated with the latter in the contest was Charles C. Pinckney, of South Carolina, who was named for the Vice-Presidency; while the Republican candidate for the minor post was Aaron Burr, an able but unscrupulous politician of New York. When the electoral votes were counted, Jefferson and Burr, it was found, had each received seventy-three votes; while Adams secured sixty-five and Pinckney sixty-four votes. The tie between Jefferson and Burr caused the election to be thrown into the House of Representatives, where the Federalists were still strong, and who, in their dislike of Jefferson, reckoned on finally giving the Presidency to Burr. To this, Hamilton, however, magnanimously objected, and in the end Jefferson secured the Presidential prize, while to Burr fell the Vice-Presidency.

For the next eight years, until the coming of Madison's Administration, Jefferson was at the helm of national affairs, assisted by an able Cabinet, the chief members of which were James Madison, Secretary of State, and the Swiss financier, Albert Gallatin, Secretary of the Treasury. Aaron Burr, as we have recorded, was Vice-President, though the relations of Jefferson with him were far from cordial, owing to his political intrigues, which led the President ultimately to eschew him and distrust his character. Jefferson's attitude toward the man was later on shown to be well justified, as the result of Burr's hateful quarrel with Alexander Hamilton, and his mortally wounding that eminent statesman in a duel, which doomed him to political and social ostracism. It was still further intensified by Burr's treasonable attempt to seduce the West out of the Union and to found with it and Mexico a rival Republic, with the looked-for aid of Britain. These unscrupulous acts occurred in Jefferson's second term; and, failing in his conspiracy, Burr deservedly brought upon himself national obloquy, as well as prosecution for treason, though nothing came of the latter.

Some two years after Jefferson's assumption of office, Ohio was admitted as a State into the Union. The next year (1803) saw, however, an enormous extension of the national domain, thanks to the President's far-seeing, if at the time unconstitutional, policy. This was the purchase from France, at the cost of $15,000,000, of Louisiana, a vast territory lying between the Mississippi, the Rocky Mountains, and the Rio Grande, which had been originally settled by the French, and by their government ceded in 1763 to Spain as a set-off for Florida, while the French King at the same time ceded his other possessions on this continent to England. In 1800, Napoleon had forced Spain to re-cede Louisiana to France, as the price of the First Consul's uncertain goodwill and other intangible or elusive favors. At this period, France desired to occupy the country, or at least to form a great seaport at New Orleans, the entrepot of the Mississippi, that might be of use to her against English warships in the region of the West Indies. When news of the transfer of Louisiana to France reached this side of the water, Jefferson was greatly exercised over it, and had notions of off-setting it by some joint action with Great Britain. His inducement to this unwonted course, considering his hatred of England and love for France, was his knowledge of the fact that French occupation of Louisiana meant the closing of the Mississippi to American commerce.

The purchase of Louisiana, which at one stroke more than doubled the existing area of the nation, was at first hotly opposed, especially by the Federalists. It was deemed by them an unwarrantable stretch of the Constitution on Jefferson's part, both in negotiating for it as a then foreign possession without authority from Congress, and in pledging the country's resources in its acquisition. The President was, however, sustained in his act, not only by the Senate, which ratified the purchase, but by the hearty approval and acclaim of the people. Happily at this time the nation was ready for the acquisition and in good shape financially to pay for it, since the country was prospering, and its finances, thanks to the President's policy of economy and retrenchment, were adequate to assume the burden involved in the purchase. The national debt at this period was being materially reduced, and with its reduction came, of course, the saving on the interest charge; while the national income and credit were encouragingly rising. Though the economical condition of the United States was thus favorable at this era, the state of trade, hampered by the policy of commercial restriction against foreign commerce, then prevailing, was not as satisfactory as the shippers of the East and the commercial classes desired. The reason of this was the unsettled relations of the United States with foreign countries, and especially with England, whose policy had been and still was to thwart the New World republic and harass its commerce and trade. To this England was incited by the bitter memories of the Revolutionary war and her opposition to rivalry as mistress of the seas. Hence followed, on the part of the United States, the non-Importation Act, the Embargo Act of 1807-08, and other retaliatory measures of Jefferson's administration, coupled with reprisals at sea and other expedients to offset British empressment of American sailors and the right of search, so ruthlessly and annoyingly put in force against the newborn nation and her maritime people. The English people themselves, or a large proportion of them at least, were as strongly opposed to these aggressions of their government as were Americans, and while their voice effected little in the way of amelioration, it brought the two peoples once more distinctly nearer to the resort to war. Meanwhile, the Embargo Act had become so irritating to our own people that the Jefferson administration was compelled to repeal it, though saving its face, for the time being, by the enforcement of the non-intercourse law, which imposed stringent restrictions upon British and French ships entering American harbors.

Such are the principal features of the Jefferson administration and the more important questions with which it had to deal. Among other matters which we have not noted were the organization of the United States Courts; the removal of the seat of government from Philadelphia to Washington; the party complexion of Jefferson's appointments to the civil service, in spite of his expressed design to be non-partisan in the selection to office; and the naming of men for the foreign embassies, such as James Monroe as plenipotentiary to France, assisted at the French Court by Robert R. Livingstone, and at the Spanish Court by Charles C. Pinckney. Other matters to which Jefferson gave interested attention include the dispatch of the explorers, Lewis and Clarke, to report on the features of the Far Western country, then in reality a wilderness, and to reclaim the vast unknown region for civilization. The details of this notable expedition up the Missouri to its source, then on through the Indian country across the Rockies to the Pacific, need not detain us, since the story is familiar to all. With the Louisiana purchase, it opened up great tracts of the continent, later on to become habitable and settled areas, and make a great and important addition to the public domain. In the appointment of the expedition and the interest taken in it, Jefferson showed his intelligent appreciation of what was to become of high value to the country, and ere long result in a land of beautiful homes to future generations of its hardy people.

At the close of his second term in the Presidential chair (1809) Jefferson retired once more, and finally, to "Monticello," after over forty years of almost continuous public service. His career in this high office was entirely worthy of the man, being that of an honorable and public-spirited, as well as an able and patriotic, statesman. If not so astute and sagacious as some who have held the presidency, especially in failing to see where his political principles, if carried out to their logical conclusions, would lead, his conscientiousness and liberality of mind prevented him from falling gravely into error or making any very fatal mistakes. Though far from orthodox,—indeed, a freethinker he may be termed, in matters of religious belief, his personal life was most exemplary, and his relations with his fellowmen were ever just, honorable, and upright. He had no gifts as a speaker, but was endowed highly as a writer and thinker; and, generally, was a man of broad intelligence, unusual culture for his time, and possessed a most alert and enlightened mind. His interest in education and the liberal arts was great, and with his consideration for the deserving poor and those in class servitude, was indulged in at no inconsiderable cost to his pocket. His hospitality was almost a reproach to him, as his impoverished estates and diminished fortunes in the latter part of his life attest. His faith in democracy as a form of government was unbounded, as was his loyalty to that beneficent political creed summed up in the motto— "Liberty, Equality, and Fraternity." "As a president," writes the lecturer, Dr. John Lord, "he is not to be compared with Washington for dignity, for wisdom, for consistency, or executive ability. Yet, on the whole, he has left a great name for giving shape to the institutions of his country, and for intense patriotism."

"Jefferson's manners," records the same entertaining writer, "were simple, his dress was plain, he was accessible to everybody, he was boundless in his hospitalities, he cared little for money, his opinions were liberal and progressive, he avoided quarrels, he had but few prejudices, he was kind and generous to the poor and unfortunate, he exalted agricultural life, he hated artificial splendor, and all shams and lies. In his morals he was irreproachable, unlike Hamilton and Burr; he never made himself ridiculous, like John Adams, by egotism, vanity, and jealousy; he was the most domestic of men, worshipped by his family and admired by his guests; always ready to communicate knowledge, strong in his convictions, perpetually writing his sincere sentiments and beliefs in letters to his friends,—as upright and honest a man as ever filled a public station, and finally retiring to private life with the respect of the whole nation, over which he continued to exercise influence after he had parted with power. And when he found himself poor and embarrassed in consequence of his unwise hospitality, he sold his library, the best in the country, to pay his debts, as well as the most valuable part of his estate, yet keeping up his cheerfulness and serenity of temper, and rejoicing in the general prosperity,—which was produced by the ever-expanding energies and resources of a great country, rather than by the political theories which he advocated with so much ability."

In Jefferson's own mind, just what was the essence of his political gospel we ascertain from a succinct yet comprehensive passage in his able First Inaugural Address. In that address President Jefferson sets forth instructively what he terms the essential principles of government, and those upon which, as he conceives, his own administration was founded and by which it was guided. The governing principles it affirms are:— "Equal and exact justice to all men, of whatever state or persuasion, religious or political; peace, commerce, and honest friendship with all nations, entangling alliances with none; the support of the state governments in all their rights, as the most competent administrations for our domestic concerns, and the surest bulwarks against anti-republican tendencies; the preservation of the general government in its whole constitutional vigor, as the sheet-anchor of our peace at home and safety abroad; a jealous care of the right of election by the people; a mild and safe corrective of abuses which are lopped by the sword of revolution, where peaceable remedies are unprovided; absolute acquiescence in the decisions of the majority, the vital principle of republics, from which is no appeal but to force, the vital principle and immediate parent of despotism; a well-disciplined militia, our best reliance in peace and for the first moments of war, till regulars may relieve them; the supremacy of the civil over the military authority — economy in the public expenditure, that labor may be lightly burdened; the honest payment of our debts, and sacred preservation of the public faith; encouragement of agriculture, and of commerce as its handmaiden; the diffusion of information and arraignment of all abuses at the bar of the public reason; freedom of religion, freedom of the press, and freedom of person, under the protection of the Habeas Corpus; and trial by juries impartially selected. These principles form the bright constellation which has gone before us, and guided our steps through an age of revolution and reformation. The wisdom of our sages and the blood of our heroes have been devoted to their attainment; they should be the creed of our political faith; the text of civic instruction; the touchstone by which to try the services of those we trust; and should we wander from them in moments of error or of alarm, let us hasten to retrace our steps and regain the road which alone leads to peace, liberty, and safety."

Jefferson had completed his sixty-sixth year when he relinquished the presidency to his friend and pupil, James Madison, and retired to his loved Virginia home. There he lived on for seventeen years, enjoying the esteem and respect of the nation, and taking active interest in his favorite schemes on behalf of education in his native state and his helpful work in founding the college which was afterwards expanded into the University of Virginia. His interest in national affairs, up to the last, remained keen and fervid, as the vast collection of his published correspondence show, as well as his many visiting contemporaries attest. In the winter of 1825-6, his health began to fail, and in the following spring he made his will and prepared for posterity the original draft of his great historic achievement as a writer and patriot—the Declaration of Independence. As the year (1826) wore on, he expressed a wish to live until the fiftieth anniversary of the nation's independence, a wish that, as in the case of his distinguished contemporary, John Adams, was granted by the favor of Heaven, and he died on the 4th of July, mourned by the whole country. In numberless quarters, funeral honors were paid to his memory, the more memorable orations being that of Daniel Webster, delivered in Boston. To his tomb still come annually many reverent worshippers; while, among the historic shrines of the nation, his home at Monticello attracts ever-increasing hosts of loving and admiring pilgrims.

THOMAS JEFFERSON'S
FIRST INAUGURAL ADDRESS—1801

Friends and fellow-citizens:—Called upon to undertake the duties of the first executive office of our country, I avail myself of the presence of that portion of my fellow-citizens which is here assmbled, to express my grateful thanks for the favor with which they have been pleased to look toward me, to declare a sincere consciousness that the task is above my talents, and that I approach it with those anxious and awful presentiments which the greatness of the charge and the weakness of my powers so justly inspire. A rising nation, spread over a wide and fruitful land, traversing all the seas with the rich productions of their industry, engaged in commerce with nations who feel power and forget right, advancing rapidly to destinies beyond the reach of mortal eye when I contemplate these transcendent objects, and see the honor, the happiness, and the hopes of this beloved country committed to the issue and the auspices of this day, I shrink from the contemplation and humble myself before the magnitude of the undertaking. Utterly, indeed, should I despair, did not the presence of many whom I here see, remind me that in the other high authorities provided by our Constitution, I shall find resources of wisdom, of virtue, and of zeal on which to rely under all difficulties. To you then, gentlemen, who are charged with the sovereign functions of legislation, and to those associated with you, I look with encouragement for that guidance and support, which may enable us to steer with safety the vessel in which we are all embarked amidst the conflicting elements of a troubled world.

During the contest of opinions through which we have passed, the animation of discussions and exertions has sometimes worn an aspect which might impose on strangers unused to think freely, and to speak and to write as they think. But this being now decided by the voice of the nation, enounced according to the rules of the constitution, all will, of course, arrange themselves under the will of the law, and unite in common efforts for the common good. All, too, will bear in mind this sacred principle that, though the will of the majority is in all cases to prevail, that will, to be rightful, must be reasonable; that the minority possess their equal rights, which equal laws must protect, and to violate which would be oppression.

Let us, then, fellow-citizens, unite with one heart and one mind; let us restore to social intercourse that harmony and affection without which liberty, and even life itself, are but dreary things. Let us reflect that, having banished from our land that religious intolerance under which mankind so long bled and suffered, we have yet gained little if we countenance a political intolerance as despotic, as wicked, and capable of as bitter and bloody persecution.

During the throes and convulsions of the ancient world, during the agonized spasms of infuriated man, seeking through blood and slaughter his long-lost liberty, it was not wonderful that the agitation of the billows should reach even this distant and peaceful shore; that this should be more felt and feared by some, and should divide opinion as to measures of safety. But every difference of opinion is not a difference of principle. We have called by different names brethren of the same principle. We are all republicans; we are all federalists. If there be any among us who wish to dissolve this union, or to change its republican form, let them stand undisturbed as monuments of the safety with which error of opinion may be tolerated where reason is left free to combat it.

I know, indeed, that some honest men have feared that a republican government cannot be strong; that this government is not strong enough. But would not the honest patriot, in the full tide of successful experiment, abandon a government which has so far kept us free and firm on the theoretic and visionary fear that this government, the world's best hope, may by possibility want energy to preserve itself? I trust not. I believe this, on the contrary, the strongest government on earth. I believe it is the only one where every man, at the call of the law, would fly to the standard of the law; would meet invasions of public order as his own personal concern.

Sometimes, it is said, that man cannot be trusted with the government of himself. Can he then be trusted with the government of others? Or have we found angels in the form of kings to govern him? Let history answer this question. Let us, then, pursue with courage and confidence our own federal and republican principle, our attachment to union and representative government.

Kindly separated by nature, and a wide ocean, from the exterminating havoc of one quarter of the globe, too high-minded to endure the degradation of the others; possessing a chosen country with room enough for all to the hundredth and thousandth generation; entertaining a dull sense of our equal right to the use of our own faculties, to the acquisition of our own industry, to honor and confidence from our fellow-citizens, resulting not from birth, but from our actions and their sense of them, enlightened by a benign religion, professed, indeed, and practiced in various forms, yet all of them inculcating honesty, truth, temperance, gratutude and the love of man, acknowledging and adoring an overruling Providence, which by all its dispensations proves that it delights in the happiness of man here and in his greater happiness hereafter. With all these blessings, what more is necessary to make us a happy and a prosperous people? Still one thing more, fellow-citizens: a wise and frugal government which shall restrain men from injuring one another shall leave them otherwise free to regulate their own pursuits of industry and improvement, and shall not take from the mouth of labor the bread it has earned. This is the sum of good government, and this is necessary to close the circle of our felicities.

About to enter, fellow-citizens, on the exercise of duties which comprehend everything dear and valuable to you, it is proper you should understand what I deem the essential principles of this government, and consequently those which ought to shape its administration. I will compress them in the narrowest limits they will bear, stating the general principle, but not all its limitations: Equal and exact justice to all men of whatever state or persuasion, religious or political; peace, commerce, and honest friendship with all nations, entangling alliances with none; the support of the State governments in all their rights as the most competent administrations for our domestic concerns, and the surest bulwarks against anti-republican tendencies; the preservation of the general government, in its whole constitutional vigor, as the sheet anchor of our peace at home and safety abroad; a jealous care of the right of election by the people, a mild and safe corrective of abuses, which are lopped by the sword of revolution, where peaceable remedies are unprovided; absolute acquiescence in the decisions of the majority, the vital principle of republics, from which there is no appeal but to force, the vital principle and immediate parent of despotism; a well-disciplined militia, our best reliance in peace, and for the first moments of war till regulars may relieve them; the supremacy of the civil over the military authority; economy in public expense that labor may be lightly burdened; the honest payment of our debts and sacred preservation of the public faith; encouragement of agriculture, and of commerce as its handmaid; the diffusion of information and arraignment of all abuses at the bar of the public reason; freedom of religion, freedom of the press, and freedom of person under the protection of the habeas corpus; and trial by juries impartially selected.

These principles form the bright constellation which has gone before us, and guided our steps through an age of revolution and reformation: the wisdom of our sages and the blood of our heroes have been devoted to their attainment; they should be the creed of our political faith, the text of civic instruction, the touchstone by which to try the services of those we trust; and should we wander from them in error or alarm, let us hasten to retrace our steps and to regain the road which alone leads to peace, liberty, and safety.

I repair then, fellow-citizens, to the post which you have assigned me. With experience enough in subordinate stations to know the difficulties of this, the greatest of all, I have learnt to expect that it will rarely fall to the lot of imperfect man to retire from this station with the reputation and the favor which bring him into it. Without pretensions to that high confidence you reposed in our first and greatest revolutionary character, whose preeminent services had entitled him to the first place in his country's love, and had destined for him the fairest page in the volume of faithful history, I ask so much confidence only as may give firmness and effect to the legal administration of your affairs. I shall often go wrong through defect of judgment; when right, I shall often be thought wrong by those whose positions will not command a view of the whole ground. I ask your indulgence for my errors, which will never be intentional; and your support against the errors of others, who may contemn what they would not, if seen in all its parts.

The approbation implied by your suffrage is a great consolation to me for the past; and my future solicitude will be to retain the good opinion of those who have bestowed it in advance to conciliate that of others by doing them all the good in my power, and to be instrumental to the happiness and freedom of all. Relying, then, on the patronage of your good will, I advance with obedience to the work, ready to retire from it whenever you become sensible how much better choice it is in your power to make. And may that infinite Power which rules the destinies of the universe lead our councils to what is best and give them a favorable issue for your peace and prosperity.

THE LOUISIANA PURCHASE
BY ISIDORE A. ZACHARIAS

From "Self-Culture" Magazine for Jan., 1896 by kind permission of the publishers The Werner Co., Akron, O.

No surer or more lasting cause conduced to the political, financial, and national development of this country, no unforeseen or long-sought measure received more universal approbation and revealed to all its great importance, than did the Louisiana purchase. Its acquisition marks a political revolution,—a bloodless and tearless revolution. It gave incomputable energy to the centralization of our Government. By removing the danger of foreign interference and relieving the burden of arming against hostile forces, it opened a field for the spread and growth of American institutions. It enlarged the field of freedom's action to work out the task of civilization on a basis of substantial and inspiring magnitude. It extended the jurisdiction of the United States to take in the mighty Mississippi. It gave an impetus to exploration and adventure, to investment and enterprise, and fed the infantile nation with a security born of greatness.

The expeditions of La Salle furnished the basis of the original French claims to the vast region called by France in the New World Louisiana. Settlement was begun in 1699. French explorers secured the St. Lawrence and Mississippi rivers, the two main entrances to the heart of America. They sought to connect Canada and Louisiana by a chain of armed towns and fortified posts, which were sparsely though gradually erected.

In 1722 New Orleans was made the capital of the French possessions in the Southwest. France hoped to build in this colony a kingdom rich and lucrative, and this hope the early conditions, the stretch of fertile and easily traversable country, stimulated. The French and Indian wars came on. The English forces, aided by American colonists of English descent, captured the French forts, destroyed their towns, and took dominion of their territory. The Seven Years' War, ending in America in the capture of Quebec by the immortal Wolfe, completed the downfall of French-America. The treaty of Paris ceded to Spain the territory of Louisiana.

The Government at Madrid now assumed control of the region; settlers became more numerous, the planting of sugar was begun, the province flourished. While Spain in 1782-83 occupied both sides of the Mississippi from 31 north latitude to its mouth, the United States and Great Britian declared in the Treaty of Paris that the navigation of that river from its source to its outlet should be free to both nations. Spain denied that such provisions were binding on her. She sought to levy a duty on merchandise transported on the river. She denied the right of our citizens to use the Mississippi as a highway, and complications ensued. The Americans claimed the free navigation of the river and the use of New Orleans for a place of deposit as a matter of right. However, the unfriendly policy of Spain continued for some years. In 1795 the Spanish Government became involved in a war with France. Weakened by loss of forces and fearing hostilities from this country, Spain consented to sign a treaty of friendship, boundaries and navigation with our envoy, Thomas Pinckney. Its most important article was to this effect, that "His Catholic Majesty likewise agrees that the navigation of the said river (Mississippi), in its whole breadth, from its source to the ocean, shall be free only to his subjects and to the subjects of the United States."

On October 1,1800, by the secret treaty of San Ildefonso, Spain gave back to France that province of Louisiana which in 1762 France had given her. The consideration for its retrocession was an assurance by France that the Duke of Palma, son-in-law of the King of Spain, should be raised to the dignity of King and have his territory enlarged by the addition of Tuscany. Rumors of this treaty reached America in the spring of 1801, though its exact terms were not known until the latter part of that year. Immediately upon the reception of this information, our Government and its citizens were aroused. The United States found herself hemmed in between the two professional belligerents of Europe—a perilous position for the young power. The excitement increased when, in October, 1802, the Spanish Intendant declared that New Orleans could no longer be used as a place of deposit. Nor was any other place designated for such purpose, although in the reaty [sic] of 1795 it was stipulated that in the event of a withdrawal of the right to use New Orleans, some other point would be named. It was now a subject of extreme importance to the Republic into whose control the highway of traffic should pass. President Jefferson called the attention of Congress to this retrocession. He anticipated the French designs. He justly feared that Napoleon Bonaparte would seek to renew the old colonial glories of France, and the warlike genius and ambitious spirit of the "First Consul" augmented this fear. Word came in November, 1802, of an expedition being fitted out under French command to take possession of Louisiana, all protests of our Minister to the transfer having proved futile. Our nation then realized fully the peril of the situation. Congress directed the Governors of the States to call out 80,000 militia, if necessary, and it appropriated $2,000,000 for the purchase of the Island of New Orleans and the adjacent lands.

Early in January, 1803, the President decided to hasten matters by sending James Monroe to France, to be associated with Robert R. Livingston, our minister to that country, as commissioners for the purchase of New Orleans and the Floridas. Livingston had been previously working on the same line, but without success. Instructions were given them that if France was obstinate about selling the desired territory, to open negotiations with the British Government, with a view to preventing France from taking possession of Louisiana. European complications, however, worked in favor of this country more than did our own efforts. Ere Monroe arrived at his destination disputes arose between England and France concerning the Island of Malta. The clouds of war began to gather. Napoleon discerned that England's powerful navy would constantly menace and probably capture New Orleans, if it were possessed by him, and fearing a frustration of his designs of conquest by too remote accessions, Napoleon, at this juncture, made overtures for a sale to the United States not only of the Island of New Orleans but of the whole area of the province. The money demanded would be helpful to France, and the wily Frenchman probably saw in such a transfer an opportunity of embroiling the Government at Washington in boundary disputes with the British and Spanish soverigns. These considerations served to precipitate French action.

Marbois, who had the confidence of Napoleon, and who had been in the diplomatic service in America, was now at the head of the French Treasury. He was put forward to negotiate with our representatives with respect to the proposed sale. On April 10, 1803, news came from London that the peace of Amiens was at an end; war impended. Bonaparte at once sent for Marbois and ordered him to push the negotiations with Livingston, without awaiting the arrival of Monroe, of whose appointment the "First Consul" was aware. Monroe reached Paris on the 12th of April, and the negotiations, already well under way, progressed rapidly. A treaty and two conventions were signed by Barbe-Marbois for the French, and by Livingston and Monroe for the United States, on April 30th, less than three weeks after the commission had begun its work. The price agreed upon for the cession of Louisiana was 75,000,000 francs, and for the satisfying of French spoliation claims due to Americans was estimated at $3,750,000. The treaty was ratified by Bonaparte in May, 1803, and by the United States Senate in the following October. The cession of the territory was contained in one paper, another fixed the amount to be paid and the mode of payment, a third arranged the method of settling the claims due to Americans.

The treaty did not attempt a precise description or boundary of the territory ceded. In the treaty of San Ildefonso general terms only are used. It speaks of Louisiana as of "the same extent that it now has in the hands of Spain, and that it had when France possessed it, and such as it should be after the treaties subsequently entered into between Spain and the other States." The treaty with the United States describes the land as "the said territory, with all its rights and appurtenances, as fully and in the same manner as have been acquired by the French Republic, in virtue of the above-mentioned treaty concluded with his Catholic Majesty."

The Court at Madrid was astounded when it heard of the cession to the United States. Florida was left hemmed in and an easy prey in the first hostilities. Spain filed a protest against the transfer, claiming that by express provision of the articles of cession to her, France was prohibited from alienating it without Spanish consent. The protest being ignored, Spain began a course of unfriendly proceedings against the United States. Hostile acts on her part were continued to such an extent that a declaration of war on the part of this country would have been justified. We relied upon the French to protect our title. At length, without any measures of force, the cavilling of Spain ceased and she acquiesced in the transfer.

Upon being confronted with the proposition of sale by Marbois, our Ministers were dazzled. They recognized the vast importance of an acceptance, yet felt their want of authority. With a political prescience and broad patriotism they overstepped all authority and concluded the treaty for the purchase of this magnificent domain. Authorized to purchase a small island and a coaling-place, they contracted for an empire. The treaty of settlement was looked upon by our representatives as a stroke of state. When the negotiations were consummated and the treaties signed and delivered, Mr. Livingston said: "We have lived long, and this is the fairest work of our lives. The treaty we have just signed will transform a vast wilderness into a flourishing country. From this day the United States becomes a first-class power. The articles we have signed will produce no tears, but ages of happiness for countless human beings." Time has verified these expressions. At the same period, the motives and sentiment of Bonaparte were bodied forth in the sentence: "I have given to England a maritime rival that will sooner or later humble her pride."

The acquisition was received with merited and general applause. Few objections were made. The only strenuous opposition arose from some Federalists, who could see no good in any act of the Jeffersonian administration, however meritorious it might be. Out of the territory thus acquired have been carved Louisiana, Missouri, Kansas, Arkansas, Nebraska, Iowa, North Dakota, South Dakota, Montana, and the largest portion of Minnesota, Wyoming, and Colorado. They now form the central section of the United States, and are the homes of millions and the sources of countless wealth.

It is possible here to notice but briefly the vast and permanent political and economical consequences to the United States of this purchase. The party which performed this service came into power as the maintainer of voluntary union. The soul of the strict construction party was Thomas Jefferson. Inclined to French ideas, he had been for several years previous to the founding of our Constitution imbibing their extreme doctrines. No sooner did he return than he discerned, with the keen glance of genius, what passed Hamilton and Adams unobserved, the key to the popular fancy. He knew precisely where the strength of the Federalists lay, and by what means alone that strength could be overpowered.

Coming into office as the champion of "State-rights and strict construction," it was beyond his power to give theoretical affirmance to this transcendent act of his agents. His own words reveal his anomalous situation: "The Constitution has made no provision for our holding foreign territory, still less for incorporating foreign nations into our Union. The executive, in seizing the fugitive occurrence which so much advances the good of their country, have done an act beyond the Constitution. The Legislature, in casting behind metaphysical subleties and risking themselves like faithful servants, must ratify and pay for it, and throw themselves on their country for doing for them unauthorized what we know they would have done for themselves had they been in a position to do it." "Doing for them unauthorized what we know they would have done for themselves" was the policy of the Federalists, and the very ground upon which Mr. Jefferson had denounced their policy and defeated them. The purchase was, in fact, quite within those implied powers of the Constitution which had always been contended for by the Federalists, and such leaders as Hamilton and Morris acknowledged this. Under the strict construction theory, not only could there be no authority for such an acquisition of territory without the consent of the several States denominated "part of the original compact," but the manifest and necessary consequences of this accession, in its effects upon the Union and upon the balance of power within the Government, were overwhelming to such an extent as to amount almost to a revolution.

This event may be looked upon as a revolution in the direction of unification and the impairment of the powers of the several States, brought about by the very party which had undertaken to oppose such tendencies. The territory gained stretches over a million square miles equal in area to the territory previously comprised in the Union, and twice as large as that actually occupied by the original thirteen States. Compared with this innovation, the plans of the Federalists for strengthening the Central Government were inconsiderable. A new nation was engrafted on the old, and neither the people of the several States nor their immediate representatives were questioned; but by a treaty the President and the Senate changed the whole structure of the territory and modified the relations of the States. Thenceforth, the Louisiana purchase stood as a repudiation by their own champions of the strict construction fallacies. Thenceforth, the welfare of the country stands above party allegiance. The right to make purchases was thereafter, by general acquiescence of all political parties, within the powers of the Federal Government. Indeed, it became manifest that implied as well as expressed powers accrued to the National Government.

The territory of Louisiana proved a fruitful soil for the spread of slavery, nor was it less productive of struggles and strife over the admission of States carved therefrom. The Civil War has pacified the jarring elements and left to be realized now the beneficent results of the empire gained. With Louisiana the United States gained control of the entire country watered by the Mississippi and its effluents. With the settlement of the western country, the Mississippi river assumed its normal function in the national development, forming out of that region the backbone of the Union. The Atlantic and Pacific States can never destroy the Union while the Central States remain loyal. Thus do we see the basis of our governmental existence removed from the narrow strip along the Atlantic to the far larger central basin; binding by natural ligaments a union far less secure on mere constitutional or artificial connections. Thus have the intentions of its projectors been fulfilled, the peace of our nation secured, a spirit of confidence in our institutions diffused, and enterprise and prosperity advanced. The purchase was an exercise of patriotism unrestrained and unbiased by considerations unconnected with the public good. It curbed the impulse of State jealousies, secured to the Union unwonted prestige, and discovered the latent force and broad possibilities of our national system.

ANECDOTES AND CHARACTERISTICS OF JEFFERSON

JEFFERSON'S BRIDAL JOURNEY.

Jefferson and his young bride, after the marriage ceremony, set out for their Monticello home. The road thither was a rough mountain track, upon which lay the snow to a depth of two feet.

At sunset they reached the house of one of their neighbors eight miles distant from Monticello. They arrived at their destination late at night thoroughly chilled with the cold.

They found the fires all out, not a light burning, not a morsel of food in the larder, and not a creature in the house. The servants had all gone to their cabins for the night, not expecting their master and mistress.

But the young couple, all the world to each other, made merry of this sorry welcome to a bride and bridegroom, and laughed heartily over it.

WOULD MAKE NO PROMISES FOR THE PRESIDENCY.

While the Presidential election was taking place in the House of Representatives, amid scenes of great excitement, strife and intrigue, which was to decide whether Jefferson or Burr should be the chief magistrate of the nation, Jefferson was stopped one day, as he was coming out of the Senate chamber, by Gouverneur Morris, a prominent leader of the Federalists.

Mr. Morris said, "I wish to have an earnest talk with you, Mr. Jefferson, on the alarming situation of things."

"I am very glad," said Jefferson, "to talk matters over with you."

"As you well know," said Mr. Morris, "I have been strenuously opposing you, as have also the large minority of the States."

"To be frank with you," he continued, "we are very much afraid of you."

"We fear,

"First—That you will turn all the Federalists out of office.

"Second—That you will put down the navy.

"Third—That you will wipe off the public debt

"Now, if you will declare, or authorize your friends to declare that you will not take these steps, your election will be made sure."

Mr. Jefferson replied, "Gouverneur Morris, I naturally want to be President, and yet I cannot make any terms to obtain the position.

"I shall never go into the office by capitulation. I cannot have my hands tied by any conditions which would hinder me from pursuing the measures which I deem best for the public good.

"I must be perfectly free. The world can judge my future

course by that which I have hitherto followed.

"I am thankful to you for your interest, but I cannot make the slightest promise."

THE MOULD-BOARD OF LEAST RESISTANCE.

Mr. A. J. Stansbury says: "I heard John Randolph (who hated Jefferson) once describe, in his own biting, caustic manner, the delight expressed by him in a new model for the mould-board of a plough.

"It was called 'the mould-board of least resistance;' and the inventor had gone into a very profound mathematical demonstration, to prove that it deserved its name.

"Jefferson listened and was convinced; and deeming it a great discovery, recommended it, with zeal, to all his agricultural friends.

"The Virginia planters, accordingly (who thought every thing of their great man as a natural philosopher), agreed, many of them, to take this new 'mould-board of least resistance.'

"It was accordingly cast, and forwarded to their farms; when lo! on trial, no ordinary team could draw it through the soil."

JEFFERSON AS AN INVENTOR.

"He sometimes figured as an inventor himself, and on that subject let me relate to you an anecdote which vividly portrays the character of his mind. You know that he had perched his country seat on a mountain height, commanding a magnificent prospect, but exposed to the sweep of wintry winds, and not very convenient of access.

"Not far from Monticello, and within the bounds of his estate, was a solitary and lofty hill, so situated as to be exposed to the blast of two currents of wind, coming up through valleys on different sides of it.

"Mr. Jefferson thought this would be an admirable position for a wind-mill; and having recently invented a model for a saw-mill to be moved by vertical sails, he sent for an engineer and submitted it to his judgment. "The man of professional science examined his plan, and listened with profound attention and deference to Mr. Jefferson's explanations of it, and to his eloquent illustration of the advantages it would secure.

"He very attentively heard him through, but made no comment upon the plan.

" 'What do you think of my idea?' said Mr. Jefferson.

"'I think it is a most ingenious one,' was the reply, 'and decidedly the best plan for a saw-mill I have ever seen.'

"Jefferson was delighted, and forthwith entered into a written agreement for the erection of such a mill on the neighboring height.

"The work went bravely on; the inventor very frequently mounting his horse, and riding over to see how it proceeded.

"When the frame was up, and the building approached its completion, the engineer rode over to Monticello to obtain a supply of money, and to get some directions about the saws.

"Jefferson kept him to dinner; and when the cloth was removed and wine sat upon the table, he turned to his guest, and with an air of much satisfaction, exclaimed,

" 'And so, Mr.——, you like my mill.'

" 'I do, sir, indeed, very much; it is certainly one of the greatest improvements in the construction of saw mills I ever witnessed.'

" 'You think the sails are so hung that it cannot fail to work?'

" 'Certainly; it must work, it cannot help it.'

" 'And there's always a wind upon that hill; if it does not come up one valley, it is sure to come up the other; and the hill is so high and steep that there is nothing to interrupt the full sweep of the wind, come which way it will. You think, then, on the whole, that the thing cannot fail of complete success?'

" 'I should think so, sir, but for one thing.'

" 'Ah! What's that?'

" 'I have been wondering in my own mind, how you are to get up your saw-logs.'

"Jefferson threw up his hands and eyes: 'I never thought of that!'

"The mill was abandoned, of course."

JEFFERSON AND THE JOCKEY.

"Jefferson's favorite exercise was riding. He was a judge of a horse, and rode a very good one.

"One day, during his presidential term, he was riding somewhere in the neighborhood of Washington, when there came up a cross road, a well-known jockey and dealer in horse-flesh, whose name we will call Jones.

"He did not know the President, but his professional eye was caught, in a moment, by the noble steed he rode.

"Coming up with an impudent boldness characteristic of the man, he accosted the rider, and forthwith began talking in the slang of his trade, about the horse, his points, his age, and his value, and expressed a readiness to 'swap' horses.

"Mr. Jefferson gave him brief replies, and civilly declined all offers of exchange.

"The fellow offered boot, and pressed and increased his bids, as the closer he looked at the stranger's steed, the better he liked him.

"All his offers were refused with a coolness that nettled him.

"He then became rude, but his vulgarity made as little impression as his money, for Jefferson had the most perfect command of his temper, and no man could put him in a passion.

"The jockey wanted him to show the animal's gait, and urged him to trot with him for a wager. But all in vain.

"At length, seeing that the stranger was no customer, and utterly impracticable, he raised his whip and struck Mr. Jefferson's horse across the flank, setting him off in a sudden gallop, which would have brought a less accomplished rider to the ground.

"At the same time he put spurs to his own beast, hoping for a race. Jefferson kept his seat, reined in his restive steed, and put an equally effective rein upon his own temper.

"The jockey wondered; but impudently turned it off with a laugh, and still keeping by the side of his new acquaintance, began talking politics. Being a staunch Federalist, he commenced to launch out against 'Long Tom,' and the policy of his administration.

"Jefferson took his part in the conversation, and urged some things in reply.

"Meanwhile they had ridden into the city, and were making their way along Pennsylvania avenue. At length they came opposite the gate of the presidential mansion.

"Here Mr. Jefferson reined up, and courteously invited the man to enter.

"The jockey raised his eye-brows, and asked—

" 'Why, do you live here?'

" 'Yes,' was the simple reply.

" 'Why, stranger, what the deuce might be your name?'

" 'My name is Thomas Jefferson.'

"Even the jockey's brass turned pale—when, putting spurs to his nag, he exclaimed—

" 'And my name is Richard Jones, and I'm ok!'

"Saying which, he dashed up the avenue at double quick time, while the President looked after him with a smile, and then rode into the gate."

JEFFERSON AND PATRICK HENRY.

Patrick Henry was an early friend and companion of Jefferson. He was a jovial young fellow noted for mimicry, practical jokes, fiddling and dancing. Jefferson's holidays were sometimes spent with Henry, and the two together would go off on hunting excursions of which each was passionately fond. Both were swift of foot and sound of wind.

Deer, turkey, foxes and other game were eagerly pursued. Jefferson looked upon Patrick Henry as the moving spirit of all the fun of the younger circle, and had not the faintest idea of the wonderful talents that lay latent in his companion's mind.

And, Henry too, did not see in the slender, freckled, sandy-haired Jefferson, the coming man who was to be united with him in some of the most stirring and important events in American history.

Jefferson did not realize that this rustic youngster, careless of dress, and apparently thoughtless in manner, and sometimes, to all appearance, so unconcerned that he was taken by some to be an idiot, was to be the flaming tongue of a coming Revolution. Henry did not dream that this fiddling boy, Jefferson, was to be the potent pen of a Declaration which was to emancipate a hemisphere.

One day in 1760, just after Jefferson had entered upon his college studies at Williamsburg, Henry came to his room to tell him, that since their parting of a few months before, after the Christmas holidays, he had studied law, and had come to Williamsburg to get a license to practice. The fact was he had studied law but six weeks, and yet felt himself able to pass the examination. The examination was conducted by four examiners. Three of them signed the license. The fourth, George Wythe, refused his signature. But Henry was now duly admitted to the bar. He went back, however, to assist his father-in-law, Mr. Shelton, in tending his tavern, and for four years, practicing occasionally, he waited his time.

In May, 1765, Henry was elected to the House of Burgesses which met at Williamsburg. While in attendance as a member Henry was the guest of young Jefferson. Henry presented a rustic appearance. His dress was coarse and worn. His fame had not become fully known at Williamsburg, "and he moved about the streets unrecognized though not unmarked. The very oddity of his appearance provoked comment."

In the Assembly were some of the most brilliant and distinguished men in the Colony. Among them were Peyton Randolph, George Wythe, John Robinson, Richard Henry Lee, and Edmund Pendleton.

Dignified manners prevailed among the members. An elaborate and formal courtesy characterized them in their proceedings. They were polished and aristocratic men, not specially interested in the welfare of the common people. They were strongly desirous of perpetuating the class distinctions observed in Virginia society. A very marked contrast was apparent between them and the tall, gaunt, coarse-attired, unpolished member from Louisa.

Not being personally known to the majority of the House, little notice was taken of him, and no expectaions of any particular influence to be exercised by him upon its deliberations were expected. When the news of the passage of the Stamp Act reached the assembly, amazement and indignation were felt by the Royalist leaders, at the folly of the English ministry. But there seemed no way before them but submission to the Imperial decree. But Henry saw that the hour had come for meeting the issue between the King and the Colonies.

He rose in his seat and offered his famous Five Resolutions, which in substance declared that Englishmen living in America had all the rights of Englishmen living in England, and that all attempts to impose taxes upon them without the consent of their own representatives, had "a manifest tendency to destroy British as well as American freedom."

These resolutions provoked an animated and exciting debate. There is a strong probability that Jefferson knew the intentions of Henry, for he was present on that ever memorable occasion in the House.

No provision was made in the Assembly chamber for spectators. There was no gallery from which they could look down upon the contestants. In the doorway between the lobby and the chamber Jefferson took his stand, intently watching Henry's attitude and actions.

In a hesitating way, stammering in his utterances, he began reading his Resolutions. Then followed the opening sentences of the magnificent oration of this "Demosthenes of the woods," as Byron termed him.

No promise did they give of what was to follow. Very soon the transformation came. Jefferson saw him draw himself to his full height and sweep with a conqueror's gaze the entire audience before and about him.

No impediment now; no inarticulate utterances now. With a voice rich and full, and musical, he poured out his impassioned plea for the liberties of the people. Then soaring to one of his boldest flights, he cried out in electric tones:

"Caesar had his Brutus, Charles the First his Cromwell, and George the Third -." The Speaker sprang to his feet, crying, "Treason! treason!" The whole assembly was in an uproar, shouting with the Speaker, "Treason! treason!" Not only the royalists, but others who were thoroughly alarmed by the orator's audacious words, joined in the cry. But never for a moment did Henry flinch. Fixing his eye upon the Speaker, and throwing his arm forward from his dilating form, as though to hurl the words with the power of a thunderbolt, he added in a tone none but he himself could command, "May profit by their example." Then, with a defiant look around the room, he said, "If this be treason, make the most of it."

Fifty-nine years afterwards Jefferson continued to speak of that great occasion with unabated enthusiasm. He narrated anew the stirring scenes when the shouts of; "treason, treason," echoed through the Hall.

In his record of the debate which followed the speech of Henry he described it as "most bloody." The arguments against the resolutions, he said were swept away by the "torrents of sublime eloquence" from the lips of Patrick Henry. With breathless interest, Jefferson, standing in the doorway, watched the taking of the vote on the last resolution. It was upon this resolution that the battle had been waged the hottest. It was carried by a majority of a single vote. When the result was announced, Peyton Randolph, the King's Attorney General, brushed by Jefferson, in going out of the House, exclaiming bitterly with an oath as he went, "I would have given five hundred guineas for a single vote."

The next day, in the absence of the mighty orator, the timid Assembly expunged the fifth resolution and modified the others. The Governor, however, dissolved the House for daring to pass at all the resolutions. But he could not dissolve the spirit of Henry nor the magical effect of the resolutions which had been offered. By his intrepid action Henry took the leadership of the Assembly out of the hands which hitherto had controlled it.

The resolutions as originally passed were sent to Philadelphia. There they were printed, and from that center of energetic action were widely circulated throughout the Colonies. The heart of Samuel Adams and the Boston patriots were filled with an unspeakable joy as they read them. The drooping spirits of the people were revived and the doom of the Stamp Act was sealed.

WASHINGTON AND JEFFERSON.

Dr. James Schouler says: "That Jefferson did not enter into the rhapsodies of his times which magnified the first President into a demigod infallible, is very certain; and that, sincerely or insincerely, he had written from his distant retreat to private friends in Congress with less veneration for Washington's good judgment on some points of policy than for his personal virtues and honesty, is susceptible of proof by more positive testimony than the once celebrated Mazzei letter. Yet we should do Jefferson the justice to add that political differences of opinion never blinded him to the transcendent qualities of Washington's character, which he had known long and intimately enough to appreciate with its possible limitations, which is the best appreciation of all. Of many contemporary tributes which were evoked at the close of the last century by that great hero's death, none bears reading so well in the light of another hundred years as that which Jefferson penned modestly in his private correspondence."

INFLUENCE OF PROF. SMALL ON JEFFERSON.

Speaking of the influence exerted over him by Dr. William Small, Professor of Mathematics at William and Mary College, who supplied the place of a father, and was at once "guide, philosopher and friend," Jefferson said: "It was Dr. Small's instruction and intercourse that probably fixed the destinies of my life."

JEFFERSON AND THE UNIVERSITY OF VIRGINIA.

In the epitaph of Jefferson, written by himself, there is no mention of his having been Governor of Virginia, Plenipotentiary to France, Secretary of State, Vice President and President of the United States. But the inscription does mention that he was the "Author of the Declaration of American Independence; of the Statute of Virginia for Religious Freedom; and Father of the University of Virginia."

These were the three things which, in his own opinion, constituted his most enduring title to fame. and it is to be observed that freedom was the fruit of all three. By the first he contributed to the emancipation of the American colonies from British rule; by the second he broke the chains of sectarian bigotry that had fettered his native State; and by the third he gave that State and her sisters the chance to strike the shackles of ignorance from the minds of their sons.

Free Government, free faith, free thought—these were the treasures which Thomas Jefferson bequeathed to his country and his State; and who, it may well be asked, has ever left a nobler legacy to mankind?

His was a mind that thrilled with that active, aggressive and innovating spirit which has done so much to jostle men out of their accustomed grooves and make them think for themselves.

No one appreciated more than he the fact that the light of experience, as revealed in the history of the race, should be the guide of mankind. But, for that very reason, he did not slavishly worship the past, well knowing that history points not only to the wisdom of sages and the virtues of saints, but also to the villainy of knaves and the stupidity of fools.

The condition of life is change; the cessation of change is death. History is movement, not stagnation; and Jefferson emphatically believed in progress.

The fact that a dogma in politics, theology or educational theory had been accepted by his ancestors did not make it necessarily true in his eyes. "Let well enough alone" was no maxim of his. Onward and upward was ever his aim.

His interests were wide and intense, ranging from Anglo-Saxon roots to architectural designs, from fiddling to philosophy, from potatoes to politics, from rice to religion. In all these things, and in many more besides, he took the keenest interest; but in nothing, perhaps, did he display throughout his life a more unfaltering zeal than in the cause of education.

"A system of general instruction," said he in 1818, "which shall reach every description of our citizens, from the richest to the poorest, as it was the earliest, so it will be the latest of all the public concerns in which I shall permit myself to take an interest."

From first to last Jefferson's aim was to establish, in organic union and harmonious co-operation, a system of educational institutions consisting of (1) primary schools, to be supported by local taxation; (2) grammar schools, classical academies or local colleges; and (3) a State University, as roof and spire of the whole edifice.

He did not succeed in realizing the whole of his scheme, but he did finally succeed in inducing the Legislature to pass an act in the year 1819 by which the State accepted the gift of Central College (a corporation based upon private subscriptions due to Jefferson's efforts), and converted it into the University of Virginia.

This action was taken on the report of a commission previously appointed, which had met at Rockfish Gap, in the Blue Ridge Mountains — a commission composed probably of more eminent men than had ever before presided over the birth of a university. Three of these men, who met together in that unpretentious inn, were Thomas Jefferson, James Madison and James Monroe (then President of the United States).

Yet it was remarked by the lookers-on that Mr. Jefferson was the principal object of regard both to the members and spectators; that he seemed to be the chief mover of the body—the soul that animated it; and some who were present, struck by their manifestations of deference, conceived a more exalted idea of him on this simple and unpretending occasion than they had ever previously entertained.—R. H. Dabney.

THE FINANCIAL DIARY OF THOMAS JEFFERSON.

Thomas Jefferson kept a financial diary and account book

from January 1st 1791, to December 28th, 1803, embracing the last three years of his service as Secretary of State under Washington, the four years of his Vice-Presidency under John Adams, and the first three years following his own election to the Presidency.

This diary was one of the most valuable treasures in the library of the late Mr. Tilden.

Among the items enumerated in the very fine, but neat and legible hand of Mr. Jefferson, is the following:

"Gave J. Madison ord. on bank for 9625 D."

The modern symbol of the dollar was not then in use. Jefferson uniformly used a capital D to denote this unit of our Federal currency.

Madison was Jefferson's most intimate friend, and was a member of congress at the time the above entry was made Jan. 8, 1791, at Philadelphia.

Whenever Jefferson went home to Monticello or returned thence to his duties, he frequently stopped with Mr. Madison.

While they were in the public service together, it appears by this diary, that they traveled together to and from their posts of duty. It also seems that one or the other generally acted as paymaster.

The inadequate salary of $3,500 which Jefferson received as Secretary of State, was $500 more than that of any other cabinet officer.

HORSE BACK RIDING TO INAUGURATION.

It would seem on the authority of Mrs. Randolph, the great-granddaughter of Mr. Jefferson, in her work, "The Domestic Life of Thomas Jefferson," that the President rode "the magnificent Wildair" to the capitol, and hitched to the palisades while he went in to deliver his inaugural. The truth of the incident, however, is not established.

In Jefferson's diary we have this entry:

Feb'y 3, 1801, Rec'd from Col. John Hoomes of the Bowling Green a bay horse Wildair, 7 yr. old, 16 hands high, for which I am to pay him 300 D May 1.

There were no pavements, sidewalks nor railroads then in Washington. There were not even wagon roads. There was no getting about, therefore, for either men or women without horses.

COST OF SERVANTS, ETC.

Jefferson estimated the cost of his ten servants per week, $28.70, or $2.87 per head.

Jefferson managed to pay off many of his small debts with his first year's salary as President. It seems never to have occurred to him to lay by anything out of his receipts.

He thought that at the end of the second year he had about $300 in hand.

It is interesting to know in these temperance days that the wine bill of Jefferson was $1,356.00 per year.

Mr. Jefferson, judging by his diary, was an inveterate buyer of books and pamphlets. He also apparently never missed an opportunity of seeing a show of any kind.

There are items for seeing a lion, a small seal, an elephant, an elk, Caleb Phillips a dwarf, a painting, etc., with the prices charged. It cost him 11 1/2 d for seeing the lion, and 25 cents the dwarf.

WOULD TAKE NO PRESENTS.

The Rev. Mr. Leland sent him a great cheese, presumably as a present. Mr. Jefferson was not in the habit "of deadheading at hotels," nor of receiving presents, however inconsiderable in value, which would place him under any obligation to the donor. The diary contains the following minute regarding the cheese:

1802. Gave Rev'd Mr. Leland, bearer of the cheese of 1235 Ibs weight, 200 D.

So the monster article cost the President sixteen cents a pound.

It will be a surprise to those who have been educated to associate Mr. Jefferson's name with indifference, if not open hostility, to revealed religion, to find among his expenses— some entered as charity, but most of them, exclusive of what is reported under the charity rubric— entries like the following:

1792

Nov 27 Pd Mr B a Subscription for missionaries 15 D.

1798 Feby 26 pd 5D in part of 20D Subscription for a hot-press bible

1801

June 25 Gave order on J Barnes for 25D towards fitting up a chapel.

Sept 23 pd Contribution at a Sermon 7.20

1802

April 7 Gave order on J Barnes for 50D charity in favor of the Revd Mr Parkinson towards a Baptist meeting house.

9 Gave order on J. Barnes in favr the Revd Doctr Smith towards rebuilding Princeton College 100D

1802

July 11 Subscribed to the Wilmington Academy 100D

1803

Feby 25 Gave Hamilton & Campbell ord. on J. Barnes for 100D charity to Carlisle College.

" 28 Gave Genl Winn ord. on J. Barnes for 100D charity to Jefferson Monticello Academy in S. Carolina.

March 1. Gave in charity to the Revd Mr Chambers of Alexandria for his church an order on J. Barnes for 50D

Nov 18 Gave order on J. Barnes for 100D in favor of Revd Mr Coffin for a college in Tennessee.

We doubt whether since the Presidential salary was doubled any of President Jefferson's successors has contributed as large a percentage of his salary to charitable or religious uses.

INDOLENCE.

In a letter to his daughter Martha, written in March, 1787, Jefferson writes:

"Of all the cankers of human happiness, none corrodes with so silent, yet baneful a tooth, as indolence.

"Body and mind both unemployed, our being becomes a burthen, and every object about us loathsome, even the dearest.

"Idleness begets ennui, ennui the hypochondria, and that a diseased body.

"No laborious person was ever yet hysterical.

"Exercise and application produce order in our affairs, health of body and cheerfulness of mind. These make us precious to our friends.

"It is while we are young that the habit of industry is formed. If not then, it never is afterwards.

"The future of our lives, therefore, depends on employing well the short period of youth.

"If at any moment, my dear, you catch yourself in idleness, start from it as you would the precipice of a gulf.

"You are not, however, to consider yourself as unemployed while taking exercise. That is necessary for your health, and health is the first of all objects."

TITLES OF HONOR AND OFFICE.

He wrote to one of his friends concerning this matter as follows:

"The Senate and Representatives differed about the title of President. The former wanted to style him 'His Highness, George Washington, President of the United States, and Protector of their Liberties.' I hope the terms of Excellency, Honor, Worship, Esquire, forever disappear from among us. I wish that of Mr. would follow them."

THE TERM OF THE PRESIDENCY.

Mr. Jefferson was inclined at first to have the President elected for seven years, and be thereafter ineligible. He afterwards modified his views in favor of the present system, allowing only a continuance for eight years.

Regarding a third term, he says in his autobiography: "Should a President consent to be a candidate for a third election, I trust he would be rejected on this demonstration of ambitious views."

THE CONTINENTAL CONGRESS AND LAWYERS.

Mr. Jefferson wrote in his autobiography regarding the Continental Congress in 1783:

"Our body was little numerous, but very contentious. Day after day was wasted on the most unimportant questions.

"If the present Congress errs in too much talking, how can it be otherwise, in a body to which the people send one hundred and fifty lawyers, whose trade it is to question everything, yield nothing and talk by the hour?

"That one hundred and fifty lawyers should do business together ought not to be expected."

THE DECLARATION OF INDEPENDENCE.

George Bancroft, in glowing words, speaks of this great creation of the genius of Jefferson:

"This immortal State paper, which for its composer was the

aurora of enduring fame, was 'the genuine effusion of the soul of the country at that time.'

"It was the revelation of its mind, when, in its youth, its enthusiasm, its sublime confronting of danger, it rose to the highest creative powers of which man is capable."—Bancroft's U S., vol. 8, ch. 70.

JEFFERSON AND THE MECKLENBURG DECLARATION OF INDEPENDENCE.

"On the 30th of April, 1819, some forty-three years after Jefferson's Declaration was written, there appeared in the Raleigh (N. C.) Register what purported to be a Declaration of Independence, drawn up by the citizens of Mecklenburg County, North Carolina, on May 20th, 1775. As this was nearly fourteen months before the Colonies declared their independence, and as many of the expressions in the Mecklenburg paper bore a striking resemblance to Jefferson's expressions, it excited a good deal of curiosity, and led to a discussion which has been continued to the present day. Those desirous of seeing the arguments pro and con, put in their latest and best form, will find them in two articles in the "Magazine of American History," in the January and March numbers of 1889.

"It is sufficient here to say that there was found among the British State papers, as well as in contemporaneous newspapers in this country, the original Mecklenburg paper, which was not a Declaration of Independence at all, but simply patriotic resolutions similar to those which were published in most of the Colonies at that time.

"And so the Mecklenburg Declaration takes its place with the stories of Pocahontas and of William Tell."— Boutell.

THE LOUISIANA PURCHASE.

In effecting the purchase of Louisiana, Mr. Jefferson has thus been eulogized by James G. Blaine, in his "Twenty Years of Congress:"

"Mr. Jefferson made the largest conquest ever peacefully achieved, at a cost so small that the sum expended for the entire territory does not equal the revenue which has since been collected on its soil in a single month, in time of great public peril."

JEFFERSON AND BENEDICT ARNOLD.

Benedict Arnold, with the British troops, had entered the Chesapeake in January, 1781, and sailed up the James River. He captured Richmond, the capital, then a town of less than two thousand people, and destroyed everything upon which he could lay his hands.

Jefferson summoned the militia, who came by thousands to oppose the traitor. Arnold, however, sailed down to Portsmouth and escaped.

Jefferson then urged upon General Muhlenburg the importance of picking out a few of the best men in his command "to seize and bring off the greatest of all traitors."

"I will undertake," he said, "if they are successful in bringing him off alive, that they shall receive five thousand guineas reward among them."

The effort was not made.

A MAN OF THE PEOPLE.

Jefferson mingled a great deal with the common people, especially with mechanics.

Often, when President, he would walk down to the Navy Yard early on a summer's morning, and sitting down upon an anchor or spar, would enter into conversation with the surprised and delighted shipwrights. He asked many questions of these artisans, who would take the utmost pains to satisfy his enquiries.

His political opponents believed unjustly that he did this simply for effect. They would say,

"There, see the demagogue!"

"There's long Tom, sinking the dignity of his station to get votes and court the mob."

ARISTOCRACY OF MIND.

Although Jefferson was an ardent democrat, in some sense he was also an aristocrat.

He firmly believed in an aristocracy of mind, and told John Adams that he rejoiced that nature had created such an aristocracy.

He unmistakably gave his preference to men of learning and refinement, at least he put these above other recommendations.

Mr. Jefferson, however, was not consistent with himself, for he frequently called General Washington "Your Excellency," during the war, and also when he was a private citizen at Mt. Vernon.

EVIL YOUTHFUL COMPANIONS.

Just after his college days Mr. Jefferson fell into company, as so many young men do, of a most undesirable sort.

According to his own statements it was a source of amazement even to himself that he ever escaped to be worth anything to the world. He realized in later years what a dangerous risk he had run.

READ LITTLE FICTION.

While he was an extensive reader in his early days, going into almost every field of literature, including poetry, he read very little fiction.

In fact, there was comparatively but little fiction then worth the name. Not from any sentiment of duty or moral impropriety, but from simple aversion he let it alone.

NEITHER ORATOR NOR GOOD TALKER.

Jefferson was neither an orator nor a good talker. He could not make a speech. His voice would sink downwards instead of rising upwards out of his throat.

But as regards legal learning he was in the front rank. No one was more ready than he in ably written opinions and defenses.

It was in what John Adams termed "the divine science of

politics" that Jefferson won his immortal and resplendent fame.

SELF-CONTROL.

With all his apparent tolerance and good humor, there was a great deal of the arbitrary and despotic in Mr. Jefferson's nature. Stern principle alone enabled him to keep his native imperiousness within proper bounds.

THE INFLUENCE OF JEFFERSON'S SISTER.

Among those who exerted a marked influence on Jefferson's early years was his oldest and favorite sister Jane. She was three years his senior, and was a woman of superior standing and great elevation of character. She was his constant companion when he was at home, and a sympathizing friend to whom he unlocked his heart. She was a "singer of uncommon skill and sweetness, and both were particularly fond of the solemn music used by the Church of England in the Psalms." She died in the fall of 1765, at the age of twenty-five. He cherished her memory with the warmest affection to the close of his life.

JEFFERSON A DOCTRINAIRE.

Lewis Henry Boutell, in his "Jefferson as a Man of Letters," says:

"That Jefferson, in justifying the action of the colonists, should have thought more of the metaphysical rights than historical facts, illustrates one of the marked features of his character. He was often more of a doctrinaire than a practical statesman. He reminds us of the words which Burke applied on a certain occasion to Chatham: 'For a wise man he seemed to me at that time to be governed too much by general maxims.' "

RECONCILIATION WITH JOHN ADAMS.

For many years the friendship between Jefferson and John Adams had been broken off. Mrs. Adams had become decidedly hostile in feeling towards Jefferson. But through a mutual friend, Dr. Rush, of Philadelphia, a reconciliation was fully established between them.

It was a spectacle in which the whole country greatly rejoiced, to see the intimacy restored between the two venerable men, once Presidents of the United States, and brothers in helping secure the independence of their beloved land.

Although they did not see each other face to face again, a continuous, instructive and affectionate correspondence was kept up between them. Their topics of discourse were those relating to Revolutionary times, but especially to religion.

NEGRO COLONIZATION.

Mr. Jefferson believed in the colonization of negroes to Africa, and the substitution of free white labor in their place.

He wrote to John Lynch, of Virginia, in 1811, as follows: "Having long ago made up my mind on this subject (colonization), I have no hesitation in saying that I have ever thought it the most desirable measure which could be adopted, for gradually drawing off this part of our population most advantageously for themselves as as [sic] well as for us.

"Going from a country possessing all the useful arts, they might be the means of transplanting them among the inhabitants of Africa, and would thus carry back to the country of their origin, the seeds of civilization, which might render their sojournment and sufferings here a blessing in the end to that country."

Many other eminent men have shared the same opinion, and not a few prominent leaders among the Afro-American people.

But it is now an impossibility. The American negro is in America to stay. The ever pressing problem of his relationship to the white man involves questions of education, labor, politics and religion, which will take infinite patience, insight, forbearance and wisdom to settle justly.

EDUCATING AMERICAN BOYS ABROAD.

Mr. Jefferson was a strong opponent of the practice of sending boys abroad to be educated. He says:

"The boy sent to Europe acquires a fondness for European luxury and dissipation, and a contempt for the simplicity of his own country.

"He is fascinated with the privileges of the European aristocrats, and sees with abhorrence the lovely equality which the poor enjoy with the rich in his own country.

"He contracts a partiality for aristocracy or monarchy.

"He forms foreign friendships which will never be useful to him.

"He loses the seasons of life for forming in his own country those friendships which of all others are the most faithful and permanent.

"He returns to his own country a foreigner, unacquainted with the practices of domestic economy necessary to preserve him from ruin.

"He speaks and writes his native tongue as a foreigner, and is therefore unqualified to obtain those distinctions which eloquence of the tongue and pen insures in a free country.

"It appears to me then that an American going to Europe for education loses in his knowledge, in his morals, in his health, in his habits and in his happiness."

These utterances of Jefferson apply of course only to boys in the formative period of their lives, and not to mature students who go abroad for higher culture.

THE FRENCH REVOLUTION.

Mr. Jefferson always believed the cause of the French Revolution to be just. Its horrors and excesses were the necessary evils attendant upon the death of tyranny and the birth of liberty.

Louis the XVI was thoroughly conscientious. At the age of twenty he ascended the throne, and strove to present an example of morality, justice and economy. But he had not firmness of will to support a good minister or to adhere to a good policy.

In the course of events a great demonstration of the French populace was made against the king. Thousands of persons carrying pikes and other weapons marched to the Tuileries. For four hours Louis was mobbed. He then put on a red cap to please his unwelcome visitors, who afterwards retired.

Long after the "Days of Terror" Jefferson wrote in his autobiography:

"The deed which closed the mortal course of these sovereigns (Louis XVI and Marie Antoinette), I shall neither approve nor condemn.

"I am not prepared to say that the first magistrate of a nation cannot commit treason against his country or is not amenable to its punishment. Nor yet, that where there is no written law, no regulated tribunal, there is not a law in our hearts and a power in our hands given for righteous employment in maintaining right and redressing wrong.

"I should have shut the queen up in a convent, putting her where she could do no harm."

Mr. Jefferson then declared that he would have permitted the King to reign, believing that with the restraints thrown around him, he would have made a successful monarch.

SAYINGS OF THOMAS JEFFERSON
FROM THE LIFE OF JEFFERSON, BY DR. IRELAN

MARRIAGE.

Harmony in the marriage state is the very first object to be aimed at.

Nothing can preserve affections uninterrupted but a firm resolution never to differ in will, and a determination in each to consider the love of the other as of more value than any object whatever on which a wish had been fixed.

How light, in fact, is the sacrifice of any other wish when weighed against the affections of one with whom we are to pass our whole life!

EDITORS AND NEWSPAPERS.

Perhaps an editor might begin a reformation in some such way as this: Divide his paper into four chapters, heading the 1st, Truths; 2nd, Probabilities; 3rd, Possibilities; 4th, Lies. The first chapter would be very short, as it would contain little more than authentic papers, and information from such sources as the editor would be willing to risk his own reputation for their truth. The second would contain what, from a mature consideration of all circumstances, he would conclude to be probably true. This, however, should rather contain too little than too much. The third and fourth should be professedly for those readers who would rather have lies for their money than the blank paper they would occupy.

Give up money, give up fame, give up science, give the earth itself and all it contains rather than do an immoral act.

Whenever you are to do anything, though it can never be known but to yourself, ask yourself how you would act were all the world looking at you, and act accordingly.

From the practice of the purest virtue, you may be assured you will derive the most sublime comforts in every moment of life, and in the moment of death.

Though you cannot see when you take one step, what will be the next, yet follow truth, justice, and plain dealing, and never fear their leading you out of the labyrinth in the nearest manner possible.

An honest heart being the first blessing, a knowing head is the second.

Nothing is so mistaken as the supposition that a person is to extricate himself from a difficulty by intrigue, by chicanery, by dissimulation, by trimming, by untruth, by injustice.

I would rather be exposed to the inconveniences attending too much liberty than those attending a too small degree of it.

Yet it is easy to foresee, from the nature of things, that the encroachments of the State governments will tend to an excess of liberty which will correct itself, while those of the General Government will tend to monarchy, which will fortify itself from day to day.

Responsibility is a tremendous engine in a free government.

Nothing is more certainly written in the book of fate than that these people (the slaves) are to be free.

When we see ourselves in a situation which must be endured and gone through, it is best to make up our minds to it, meet it with firmness, and accommodate every thing to it in the best way practicable.

The errors and misfortunes of others should be a school for our own instruction.

The article of dress is, perhaps, that in which economy is the least to be recommended.

All, too, will bear in mind this sacred principle, that though the will of the majority is in all cases to prevail, that will, to be rightful, must be reasonable; that the minority possess their equal rights, which equal laws must protect, and to violate which would be oppression.

A good cause is often injured more by ill-timed efforts of its friends than by the arguments of its enemies.

Persuasion, perseverance, and patience are the best advocates on questions depending on the will of others.

I hold it, that a little rebellion, now and then, is a good thing, and as necessary in the political world as storms in the physical. An observation of this truth should render honest republican governors so mild in their punishment of rebellions, as not to discourage them too much. It is a medicine necessary for the sound health of government.

No race of kings has ever presented above one man of common sense in twenty generations.

With all the defects in our Constitution, whether general or particular, the comparison of our government with those of Europe, is like a comparison of Heaven with Hell. England, like the earth, may be allowed to take the intermediate station.

I have a right to nothing, which another has a right to take away.

Educate and inform the whole mass of the people. Enable them to see that it is their interest to preserve peace and order, and they will preserve them.

When we get piled upon one another in large cities, as in Europe, we shall become corrupt as in Europe, and go to eating one another as they do there.

Health, learning, and virtue will insure your happiness; they will give you a quiet conscience, private esteem and public honor.

If I were to decide between the pleasures derived from the classical education which my father gave me, and the estate left me, I should decide in favor of the farmer.

Good humor and politeness never introduce into mixed society a question on which they foresee there will be a difference of opinion.

The general desire of men to live by their heads rather than their hands, and the strong allurements of great cities to those who have any turn for dissipation, threaten to make them here, as in Europe, the sinks of voluntary misery.

I have often thought that if Heaven had given me choice of my position and calling, it should have been on a rich spot of earth, well watered, and near a good market for the productions of the garden. No occupation is so delightful to me as the culture of the earth, and no culture comparable to that of the garden.

I sincerely, then, believe with you in the general existence of a moral instinct. I think it is the brightest gem with which the human character is studded, and the want of it as more degrading than the most hideous of the bodily deformities.

I must ever believe that religion substantially good, which produces an honest life, and we have been authorized by one (One) whom you and I equally respect, to judge of the tree by its fruit.

Where the law of majority ceases to be acknowledged there government ends, the law of the strongest takes its place, and life and property are his who can take them.

Those who labor in the earth are the chosen people of God, if ever He has a chosen people, whose breasts he has made this peculiar deposit for substantial and genuine virtue, it is the focus in which He keeps alive that sacred fire, which otherwise might escape from the face of the earth.

The wise know their weakness too well to assume infallibility; and he who knows most knows best how little he knows.

TEN CANONS FOR PRACTICAL LIFE.

1. Never put off till to-morrow what you can do today.
2. Never trouble another for what you can do yourself.
3. Never spend your money before you have it.
4. Never buy what you do not want, because it is cheap; it will be dear to you.
5. Pride costs us more than hunger, thirst and cold.
6. We never repent of having eaten too little.
7. Nothing is troublesome that we do willingly.
8. How much pain have cost us the evils which have never happened.
9. Take things always by their smooth handle.
10. When angry count ten before you speak; if very angry, a hundred.

ADAMS AND JEFFERSON
BY DANIEL WEBSTER

Discourse in Commemoration of the Lives and Services of John and Thomas Jefferson, Delivered in Faneuil Hall, August 2, 1826.

This is an unaccustomed spectacle. For the first time, fellow-citizens, badges of mourning shroud the columns and overhang the arches of this hall. These walls, which were consecrated, so long ago, to the cause of American liberty, which witnessed her infant struggles, and rung with the shouts of her earliest victories, proclaim, now, that distinguished friends and champions of that great cause have fallen. It is right that it shall be thus. The tears which flow, and the honors that are shown when the founders of the republic die, give hope that the republic itself may be immortal. It is fit, by public assembly and solemn observance, by anthem and by eulogy, we commemorate the services of national benefactors, extol their virtues, and render thanks to God for eminent blessings, early given and long continued, to our favored countrty [sic].

Adams and Jefferson are no more; and we are assembled, fellow-citizens, the aged, the middle-aged, and the young, by the spontaneous impulse of all, under the authority of the municipal government, with the presence of the chief-magistrate of the commonwealth, and others, its official representatives, the university, and the learned societies, to bear our part in those manifestations of respect and gratitude which universally pervade the land. Adams and Jefferson are no more. On our fiftieth anniversary, the great day of national jubilee, in the very hour of public rejoicing, in the midst of echoing and re-echoing voices of thanksgiving, while their own names were on all tongues, they took their flight together to the world of spirits.

If it be true that no one can safely be pronounced happy while he lives, if that event which terminates life can alone crown its honors and its glory, what felicity is here! The great epic of their lives, how happily concluded! Poetry itself has hardly closed illustrious lives, and finished the career of earthly renown, by such a consummation. If we had the power, we could not wish to reverse this dispensation of the Divine Providence. The great objects of life were accomplished, the drama was ready to be closed. It has closed; our patriots have fallen; but so fallen, at such age, with such coincidence, on such a day, that we cannot rationally lament that that end has come, which we know could not long be deferred.

Neither of these great men, fellow-citizens, could have died, at any time, without leaving an immense void in our American society. They have been so intimately, and for so long a time blended with the history of the country, and especially so united, in our thoughts and recollections, with the events of the revolution [text destroyed] the death of either would have touched the strings of public sympathy. We should have felt that one great link connecting us with former times, was broken; that we had lost something more, as it were, of the presence of the revolution itself, and of the act of independence, and were driven on, by another great remove, from the days of our country's early distinction, to meet posterity, and to mix with the future. Like the mariner, whom the ocean and the winds carry along, till he sees the stars which have directed his course and lighted his pathless way descent, one by one, beneath the rising horizon, we should have felt that the stream of time had borne us onward till another luminary, whose light had cheered us and whose guidance we had followed, had sunk away from our sight.

But the concurrence of their death on the anniversary of independence has naturally awakened stronger emotions. Both had been presidents, both had lived to great age, both were early patriots, and both were distinguished and ever honored by their immediate agency in the act of independence. It cannot but seem striking and extraordinary, that these two should live to see the fiftieth year from the date of that act; that they should complete that year; and that then, on the day which had fast linked forever their own fame with their country's glory, the heavens should open to receive them both at once. As their lives themselves were the gifts of Providence, who is not willing to recognize in their happy termination, as well as in their long continuance, proofs that our country and its benefactors are objects of His care?

Adams and Jefferson, I have said, are no more. As human beings, indeed they are no more. They are no more, as in 1776, bold and fearless advocates of independence; no more, as on subsequent periods, the head of the government; no more, as we have recently seen them, aged and venerable objects of admiration and regard. They are no more. They are dead. But how little is there of the great and good which can die! To their country they yet live, and live forever. They live in all that perpetuates the remembrance of men on earth; in the recorded proofs of their own great actions, in the offspring of their intellect, in the deep-engraved lines of public gratitude, and in the respect and homage of mankind. They live in their example; and they live, emphatically, and will live, in the influence which their lives and efforts, their principles and opinion, now exercise, and will continue to exercise, on the affairs of men, not only in their own country, but thoughout the civilized world. A superior and commanding human intellect, a truly great man, when Heaven vouchsafes so rare a gift, is not a temporary flame, burning bright for a while, and then expiring, giving place to returning darkness. It is rather a spark of fervent heat, as well as radiant light, with power to enkindle the common mass of human mind; so that when it glimmers in its own decay, and finally goes out in death, no night follows, but it leaves the world all light, all on fire, from the potent contact of its own spirit. Bacon died; but the human understanding roused by the touch of his miraculous wand to a perception of the true philosophy and the just mode of inquiring after truth, has kept on its course successfully and gloriously. Newton died; yet the courses of the spheres are still known, and they yet move on in the orbits which he saw, and described for them, in the infinity of space.

No two men now live, fellow-citizens, perhaps it may be doubted whether any two men have ever lived in one age, who, more than those we now commemorate, have impressed their own sentiments, in regard to politics and government, on mankind, infused their own opinions more deeply into the opinions of others, or given a more lasting direction to the current of human thought. Their work doth not perish with them. The tree which they assisted to plant will flourish, although they water it and protect it no longer; for it has struck its roots deep, it has sent them to the very center; no storm, not of force to burst the orb, can overturn it; its branches spread wide; they stretch their protecting arms broader and broader, and its top is destined to reach the heavens. We are not deceived. There is no delusion here. No age will come in which the American revolution will appear less than it is, one of the greatest events in human history. No age will come in which it will cease to be seen and felt, on either continent, that a mighty step, a great advance, not only in American affairs, but in human affairs, was made on the 4th of July, 1776. And no age will come we trust, so ignorant or so unjust as not to see and acknowledge the efficient agency of these we now honor in producing that momentous event.

We are not assembled, therefore, fellow-citizens, as men overwhelmed with calamity by the sudden disruption of the ties of friendship or affection, or as in despair for the republic by the untimely blighting of its hopes. Death has not surprised us by an unseasonable blow. We have, indeed, seen the tomb close, but it has closed only over mature years, over long-protracted public service, over the weakness of age, and over life itself only when the ends of living had been fulfilled. These suns, as they rose slowly and steadily, amidst clouds and storms in their ascendant, so they have not rushed from their meridian to sink suddenly in the west. Like the mildness, the serenity, the continuing benignity of summer's day, they have gone down with slow-descending, grateful, long-lingering light; and now that they are beyond the visible margin of the world, good omens cheer us from "the bright track of their fiery car!"

There were many points of similarity in the lives and fortunes of these great men. They belonged to the same profession, and had pursued its studies and its practice, for unequal lengths of time indeed, but with diligence and effect. Both were learned and able lawyers. They were natives and inhabitants, respectively, of those two of the colonies which at the revolution were the largest and most powerful, and which naturally had a lead in the political affairs of the times. When the colonies became in some degree united, by the assembling of a general congress, they were brought to act together in its deliberations, not indeed at the same time, but both at early periods. Each had already manifested his attachment to the cause of the country, as well as his ability to maintain it, by printed addresses, public speeches, extensive correspondence, and whatever other mode could be adopted for the purpose of exposing the encroachments of the British parliament, and animating the people to a manly resistance. Both, were not only decided, but early, friends of independence. While others yet doubted, they were resolved; where others hesitated, they pressed forward. They were both members of the committee for preparing the declaration of independence, and they constituted the sub-committee appointed by the other members to make the draft. They left their seats in congress, being called to other public employment, at periods not remote from each other, although one of them returned to it afterward for a short time. Neither of them was of the assembly of great men which formed the present constitution, and neither was at any time member of congress under its provisions. Both have been public ministers abroad, both vice-presidents and both presidents. These coincidences are now singularly crowned and completed. They have died together;

and they died on the anniversary of liberty.

When many of us were last in this place, fellow-citizens, it was on the day of that anniversary. We were met to enjoy the festivities belonging to the occasion, and to manifest our grateful homage to our political fathers. We did not, we could not here forget our venerable neighbor of Quincy. We knew that we were standing, at a time of high and palmy prosperity, where he had stood in the hour of utmost peril; that we saw nothing but liberty and security, where he had met the frown of power; that we were enjoying everything, where he had hazarded everything; and just and sincere plaudits rose to his name, from the crowds which filled this area, and hung over these galleries. He whose grateful duty it was to speak to us, [Hon, Joshiah Quincy] on that day, of the virtues of our fathers, had, indeed, admonished us that time and years were about to level his venerable frame with the dust. But he bade us hope that "the sound of a nation's joy, rushing from our cities, ringing from our valleys, echoing from our hills, might yet break the silence of his aged ear; that the rising blessings of grateful millions might yet visit with glad light his decaying vision." Alas! that vision was then closing forever. Alas! the silence which was then settling on that aged ear was an everlasting silence! For, lo! in the very moment of our festivities, his freed spirit ascended to God who gave it! Human aid and human solace terminate at the grave; or we would gladly have borne him upward, on a nation's outspread hands; we would have accompanied him, and with the blessings of millions and the prayers of millions, commended him. to the Divine favor.

While still indulging our thoughts, on the coincidence of the death of this venerable man with the anniversary of independence, we learn that Jefferson, too, has fallen. and that these aged patriots, these illustrious fellow-laborers, have left our world together. May not such events raise the suggestion that they are not undesigned, and that Heaven does so order things, as sometimes to attract strongly the attention and excite the thoughts of men? The occurrence has added new interest to our anniversary, and will be remembered in all time to come.

The occasion, fellow-citizens, requires some account of the lives and services of John Adams and Thomas Jefferson. This duty must necessarily be performed with great brevity, and in the discharge of it I shall be obliged to confine myself, principally, to those parts of their history and character which belonged to them as public men.

John Adams was born at Quincy, then part of the ancient town of Braintree, on the 19th of October, (old style,) 1735. He was a descendant of the Puritans, his ancestors having early emigrated from England, and settled in Massachusetts. Discovering early a strong love of reading and of knowledge, together with the marks of great strength and activity of mind, proper care was taken by his worthy father to provide for his education. He pursued his youthful studies in Braintree, under Mr. Marsh, a teacher whose fortune it was that Josiah Quincy, Jr., as well as the subject of these remarks, should receive from him his instruction in the rudiments of classical literature. Having been admitted, in 1751, a member of Harvard College, Mr. Adams was graduated, in course, in 1755; and on the catalogue of that institution, his name, at the time of his death, was second among the living alumni, being preceded only by that of the venerable Holyoke. With what degree of reputation he left the university is not now precisely known. We know only that he was a distinguished in a class which numbered Locke and Hemmenway among its members. Choosing the law for his profession, he commenced and prosecuted its studies at Worcester, under the direction of Samuel Putnam, a gentleman whom he has himself described as an acute man, an able and learned lawyer, and as in large professional practice at that time. In 1758 he was admitted to the bar, and cormmenced business in Braintree. He is understood to have made his first considerable effort, or to have attained his first signal success, at Plymouth, on one of those occasions which furnish the earliest opportunity for distinction to many young men of the profession, a jury trial, and a criminal cause. His business naturally grew with his reputation, and his residence in the vicinity afforded the opportunity, as his growing eminence gave the power, of entering on the large field of practice which the capital presented. In 1766 he removed his residence to Boston, still continuing his attendance on the neighboring circuits, and not unfrequently called to remote parts of the province. In 1770 his professional firmness was brought to a test of some severity, on the application of the British officers and Soldiers to undertake their defense, on the trial of the indictments found against them on account of the transactions of the memorable 5th of March. He seems to have thought, on this occasion, that a man can no more abandon the proper duties of his profession, than he can abandon other duties. The event proved, that, as he judged well for his own reputation, he judged well, also, for the interest and permanent fame of his country. The result of that trial proved, that notwithstanding the high degree of excitement then existing in consequence of the measures of the British government, a jury of Massachusetts would not deprive the most reckless enemies, even the officers of that standing army quartered among them which they so perfectly abhorred, of any part of that protection which the law, in its mildest and most indulgent interpretation, afforded to persons accused of crimes.

Without pursuing Mr. Adams's professional course further, suffice it to say, that on the first establishment of the judicial tribunals under the authority of the state, in 1776, he received an offer of the high and responsible station of chief-justice of the supreme court of his state. But he was destined for another and a different career. From early life, the bent of his mind was toward politics. a propensity which the state of the times, if it did not create, doubtless very much strengthened. Public subjects must have occupied the thoughts and filled up the conversation in the circles in which he then moved, and the interesting questions at that time just arising could not but sieve on a mind like his, ardent, sanguine, and patriotic. The letter, fortunately preserved, written by him at Worcester, so early as the 12th of October, 1755, is a proof of very comprehensive views, and uncommon depth of reflection, in a young man not yet quite twenty. In this letter he predicted the transfer of power, and the establishment of a new seat of empire in America; he predicted, also, the increase of population in the colonies; and anticipated their naval distinction, and foretold that all Europe combined could not subdue them. All this is said not on a public occasion or for effect, but in the style of sober and friendly correspondence, as the result of his own thoughts. "I sometimes retire," said he, at the close of the letter, "and, laying things together, form some reflections pleasing to myself. The produce of one of these reveries you have read above."* This prognostication so early in his own life, so early in the history of the country, of independence, of vast increase of numbers, of naval force, of such augmented power as might defy all Europe, is remarkable. It is more remarkable that its author should have lived to see fulfilled to the letter what could have seemed to others, at the time, but the extravagance of youthful fancy. His earliest political feelings were thus strongly American, and from this ardent attachment to his native soil he never departed.

While still living at Quincy, and at the age of twenty-four, Mr. Adams was present, in this town, on the argument before the supreme court respecting Writs of Assistance, and heard the celebrated and patriotic speech of James Otis. Unquestionably, that was a masterly performance. No flighty declamation about liberty, no superficial discussion of popular topics, it was a learned, penetrating, convincing, constitutional argument, expressed in a strain of high and resolute patriotism. He grasped the question then pending between England and her colonies with the strength of a lion; and if he sometimes sported, it was only because the lion himself is sometimes playful. Its success appears to have been as great as its merits, and its impression was widely felt. Mr. Adams himself seems never to have lost the feeling it produced, and to have entertained constantly the fullest conviction of its important effects. "I do say," he observes, "in the most solemn manner, that Mr. Otis's Oration against Writs of Assistance breathed into this nation the breath of life."

In 1765 Mr. Adams laid before the public, what I suppose to be his first printed performance, except essays for the periodical press, A Dissertation on the Canon and Feudal Law. The object of this work was to show that our New England ancestors, in, consenting to exile themselves from their native land, were actuated mainly by the desire of delivering themeslves [sic] from the power of the hierarchy, and from the monarchial and aristocratical political systems of the other continent, and to make this truth bear with effect on the politics of the times. Its tone is uncommonly bold and animated for that period. He calls on the people, not only to defend, but to study and understand, their rights and privileges; urges earnestly the necessity of diffusing general knowledge; invokes the clergy and the bar, the colleges and academies, and all others who have the ability and the means to expose the insidious designs of arbitrary power, to resist its approaches, and to be persuaded that there is a settled design on foot to enslave all America. "Be it remembered," says the author, "that liberty must, at all hazards, be supported. We have a right to it, derived from our Maker. But if we had not, our fathers have earned it and bought it for us, at the expense of their ease, their estates, their pleasure, and their blood. And liberty cannot be preserved without a general knowledge among the people, who have a right, from the frame of their nature, to knowledge, as their great Creator, who does nothing in vain, has given them understandings and a desire to know. But, besides this, they have a right, an indisputable, unalienable, indefeasible right, to that most dreaded and envied kind of knowledge, I mean of the character and conduct of their rulers. Rulers are no more than attorneys, agents, and trustees of the people and if the cause, the interest and trust, is insidiously betrayed or wantonly trifled away, the people have a right to revoke the authority that they themselves have deputed, and to constitute other and better agents, attorneys, and trustees."

The citizens of this town conferred on Mr. Adams his first political distinction, and clothed him with his first political trust, by electing him one of their representatives in 1770.

Before this time he had become extensively known throughout the province, as well by the part he had acted in relation to public affairs, as by the exercise of his professional ability. He was among those who took the deepest interest in the controversy with England and whether in or out of the legislature, his time and talents were alike devoted to the cause. In the years 1773 and 1774 he was chosen a councilor by the members of the general court, but rejected by Governor Hutchinson in the former of those years, and by Governor Gage in the latter.

The time was now at hand, however, when the affairs of the colonies urgently demanded united counsels. An open rupture with the parent state appeared inevitable, and it was but the dictate of prudence that those who were united by a common interest and a common danger, should protect that interest and guard against that danger, by united efforts. A general congress of delegates from all the colonies having been proposed and agreed to, the house of representatives, on the 17th of June, 1774, elected James Bowdoin, Thomas Cushing, Samuel Adams, John Adams, and Robert Treat Paine, delegates from Massachusetts. This appointment was made at Salem, where the general court had been convened by Governor Gage, in the last hour of the existence of a house of representatives under the provincial charter. While engaged in this important business, the governor, having been informed of what was passing, sent his secretary with a message dissolving the general court. The secretary, finding the door locked, directed the messenger to go in and inform the speaker that the secretary was at the door with a message from the governor. The messenger returned, and informed the secretary that the orders of the house were that the doors should be kept fast; whereupon the secretary soon after read a proclamation, dissolving the general court, upon, the stairs. Thus terminated forever, the actual exercise of the political power of England in or over Massachusetts. The four last named delegates accepted their appointments, and took their seats in congress the first day of its meeting, September 5th, 1774, in Philadelphia.

The proceedings of the first congress are well known, and have been universally admired. It is in vain that we would look for superior proofs of wisdom, talent, and patriotism. Lord Chatham said that, for himself, he must declare that he had studied and admired the free states of antiquity, the master states of the world, but that, for solidity of reasoning, force of sagacity, and wisdom of conclusion, no body of men could stand in preference to this congress. It is hardly inferior praise to say that no production of that great man himself can be pronounced superior to several of the papers, published as the proceedings of this most able, most firm, most patriotic assembly. There is, indeed, nothing superior to them in the range of political disquisition. They not only embrace, illustrate and enforce everything which political philosophy, the love of liberty, and the spirit of free inquiry had antecedently produced, but they add new and striking views of their own, and apply the whole, with irresistible force, in support of the cause which had drawn them together.

Mr. Adams was a constant attendant on the deliberations of this body, and bore an active part in its important measures. He was of the committee to state the rights of the colonies, and of that, also, which reported the Address to the King.

As it was in the continental congress, fellow-citizens, that those whose deaths have given rise to this occasion were first brought together, and called on to unite their industry and their ability in the service of the country, let us now turn to the other of these distinguished men, and take a brief notice of his life up to the period when he appeared within the walls of congress.

Thomas Jefferson descended from ancestors who had been settled in Virginia for some generations, was born near the spot on which he died, in the county of Albemarle, on the 2d of April, (old style,) 1743. His youthful studies were pursued in the neighborhood of his father's residence, until he was removed to the college of William and Mary, the highest honors of which he in due time received. Having left the college with reputation, he applied himself to the study of the law under the tuition of George Wythe, one of the highest judicial names of which that state can boast. At an early age, he was elected a member of the legislature, in which he had no sooner appeared than he distinguished himself by knowledge, capacity, and promptitude.

Mr. Jefferson appears to have been imbued with an early love of letters and science, and to have cherished a strong disposition to pursue these objects. To the physical sciences, especially, and to ancient classic literature, he is understood to have had a warm attachment, and never entirely to have lost sight of them in the midst of the busiest occupations. But the times were times for action, rather than for contemplation. The country was to be defended, and to be saved, before it could be enjoyed. Philosophic leisure and literary pursuits, and even the objects of professional attention, where [sic] all necessarily postponed to the urgent calls of the public service. The exigency of the country made the same demand on Mr. Jefferson that it made on others who had the ability and the disposition to serve it; and he obeyed the call; thinking and feeling in this respect with the great Roman orator: "Quis enim est tam cupidus in perspicienda cognoscendaque rerum nature, ut, si, ei tractanti contemplantique, res cognitione dignissmas subito sit allatum periculum discrimenque patriae, cui subvenire opitularique possit, non illa omnia relinquat atque abJiciat, etiam si dinumerare se stellas, aut metiri mundi magnitudinem posse arbitretur?"

Entering with all his heart into the cause of liberty, his ability, patriotism, and power with the pen, naturally drew upon him a large participation in the most important concerns. Wherever he was, there was found a soul devoted to the cause, power to defend and maintain it, and willingness to incur all its hazards. In 1774 he published a Summary View of the Rights of British America, a valuable production among those intended to show the dangers which threatened the liberties of the country, and to encourage the people in their defense. In June, 1775, he was elected a member of the continental Congress, as successor to Peyton Randolph, who had retired on account of ill health, and took his seat in that body on the 21st of the same month.

And now, fellow-citizens, without pursuing the biography of these illustrious men further, for the present, let us turn our attention to the most prominent act of their lives, their participation in the DECLARATION OF INDEPEN-DENCE.

Preparatory to the introduction of that important measure, a committee, at the head of which was Mr. Adams, had reported a resolution, which congress adopted the 10th of May, recommending, in substance, to all the colonies which had not already established governments suited to the exigencies of their affairs, to adopt such government as would, in the opinion of the representatives of the people, best conduce to the happiness and safety of their constituents in particular, and America in general.

This significant vote was soon followed by the direct proposition which Richard Henry Lee had the honor to submit to Congress, by resolution, on the 7th day of June. The published journal does not expressly state it, but there is no doubt, I suppose, that this resolution was in the same words when originally submitted by Mr. Lee, as when finally passed. Having been discussed on Saturday, the 8th, and Monday, the 10th of June, this resolution was on the last mentioned day postponed for further consideration to the first day of July; and at the same time, it was voted that a committee be appointed to prepare a Declaration to the effect of the resolution. This committee was elected by ballot, on the following day, and consisted of Thomas Jefferson, John Adams, Benjamin Franklin, Roger Sherman, and Robert R. Livingston.

It is usual when committees are elected by ballot, that their members are arranged in order, according to the number of votes which each has received. Mr. Jefferson, therefore, had received the highest, and Mr. Adams the next highest number of votes. The difference is said to have been but of a single vote. Mr. Jefferson and Mr. Adams, standing thus at the head of the committee, were requested by the other members to act as a sub-committee to prepare the draft; and Mr. Jefferson drew up the paper. The original draft, as brought by him from his study, and submitted to the other members of the committee, with interlineations in the handwriting of Dr. Franklin, and others in that of Mr. Adams, was in Mr. Jefferson's possession at the time of his death. The merit of this paper is Mr. Jefferson's. Some changes were made in it on the suggestion of other members of the committee, and others by congress while it was under discussion. But none of them altered the tone. the frame, the arrangement, or the general character of the instrument, As a composition, the Declaration is Mr. Jefferson's. It is the production of his mind, and the high honor of it belongs to him, clearly and absolutely.

It has sometimes been said, as if it were a derogation from the merits of this paper; that it contains nothing new; that it only states grounds of proceeding, and presses topics of argument, which had often been stated and pressed before. But it was not the object of the Declaration to produce anything new. It was not to invent reasons for independence, but to state those which governed the congress. For great and sufficient causes it was proposed to declare independence; and the proper business of the paper to be drawn was to set forth those causes, and justify the authors of the measure, in any event of fortune, to the country, and to posterity. The cause of American independence, moreover, was now to be presented to the world in such manner, if it might so be, as to engage its sympathy, to command its respect, to attract its admiration. and in an assembly of most able and distinguished men, Thomas Jefferson had the high honor of being the selected advocate of this cause. To say that he performed his great work well, would be doing him injustice. To say that he did it excellently well, admirably well, would be inadequate and halting praise. Let us rather say that he so discharged the duty assigned him, that all Americans may well rejoice that the work of drawing the title-deed of their liberties devolved on his hands.

With all its merits, there are those who have thought that there was one thing in the declaration to be regretted; and that is, the asperity and anger with which it speaks of the person of the king; the industrious ability with which it accumulates and charges upon him all the injuries which the colonies had suffered from the mother country. Possibly some degree of injustice, now or hereafter, at home or abroad, may be done to the character of Mr. Jefferson, if this part of the declaration be not placed in its proper light. Anger or resentment, certainly much less personal reproach and invective, could not properly find place in a composition of such high dignity, and of such lofty and permanent character.

A single reflection on the original ground of dispute between England and the colonies, is sufficient to remove any unfavorable impression in this respect.

The inhabitants of all the colonies, while colonies, admitted themselves bound by their allegiance to the king; but they disclaimed altogether, the authority of parliament; holding themselves, in this respect, to resemble the condition of Scotland and Ireland before the respective unions of those kingdoms with England, when they acknowledged allegiance to the same king, but each had its separate legislature. The tie, therefore, which our revolution was to break, did not subsist between us and the British parliament, or between us and the British government, in the aggregate, but directly between us and the king himself. The colonists had never admitted themselves subject to parliament. That was precisely the point of the original controversy. They had uniformly denied that parliament had authority to make laws for them. There was, therefore, no subjection to parliaments to be thrown off.** But allegiance to the king did exist, and had been uniformly acknowledged; and down to 1775, the most solemn assurances had been given that it was not intended to break that allegiance, or to throw it off. Therefore, as the direct object and only effect of the declaration, according to the principles on which the controversy had been maintained on our part, were to sever the tie of allegiance which bound us to the king, it was properly and necessarily founded on acts of the crown itself, as its justifying causes. Parliament is not so much as mentioned in the whole instrument. When odious and oppressive acts are referred to, it is done by charging the king with confederating with others, "in pretended acts of legislation," the object being constantly to hold the king himself directly responsible for those measures which were the grounds of separation. Even the precedent of the English revolution was not overlooked, and in this case as well as in that, occasion was found to say that the king had abdicated the government. Consistency with the principles upon which resistance began, and with all the previous state papers issued by congress, required that the declaration should be bottomed on the misgovernment of the king; and therefore it was properly framed with that aim and to that end. The king was known, indeed, to have acted, as in other cases, by his ministers, and with his parliament; but as our ancestors had never admitted themselves subject either to ministers or to parliament, there were no reasons to be given for now refusing obedience to their authority. This clear and obvious necessity of founding the declaration on the misconduct of the king himself gives to that instrument its personal application, and its character of direct and pointed accusation.

The declaration having been reported to congress by the committee, the resolution itself was taken up and debated on the first day of July, and again on the second on which last day, it was agreed to and adopted, in these words:

"Resolved, That these united colonies are, and of right ought to be, free and independent states; that they are absolved from all allegiance to the British crown, and that all political connection between them and the state of Great Britian is, and ought to be, totally dissolved."

Having thus passed the main resolution, congress proceeded to consider the reported draft of the declaration. It was discussed on the second, and third, and fourth days of the month, in committee of the whole, and on the last of those days, being reported from that committee, it received the final approbation and sanction of congress. It was ordered, at the same time, that copies be sent to the several states, and that it be proclaimed at the head of the army. The declaration thus published did not bear the names of the members, for as yet, it had not been signed by them. It was authenticated like other papers of the congress, by the signatures of the President and secretary. On the 19th of July, as appears by the secret journal, congress "Resolved, That the declaration, passed on the fourth, be fairly engrossed on parchment, with the title and style of 'THE UNANIMOUS DECLARATION OF THE THIRTEEN UNITED STATES OF AMERICA;' and that the same, when engrossed, be signed by every member of congress." And on the SECOND day of August following, "the declaration being engrossed, and compared at the table, was signed by the members." So that it happens, fellow-citizens, that we pay these honors to their memory on the anniversary of that day, on which these great men actually signed their names to the declaration. The declaration was thus made, that is, it passed and was adopted as an act of congress, on the fourth of July; it was then signed, and certified by the President and secretary, like other acts. The FOURTH OF JULY, therefore, is the anniversary of the declaration. But the signatures of the members present were made to it, being then engrossed on parchment, on the second day of August. Absent members afterward signed, as they came in; and indeed it bears the signatures of some who were not chosen members of congress until after the fourth of July. The interest belonging to the subject will be sufficient, I hope, to justify these details.

The congress of the revolution, fellow-citizens, sat with closed doors, and no report of its debates was ever taken. The discussion, therefore, which accompanied this great measure, has never been preserved, except in memory and by tradition. But it is, I believe, doing no injustice to others to say that the general opinion was, and uniformly has been, that in debate, on the side of independence, John Adams had no equal. The great author of the declaration himself has expressed that opinion uniformly and strongly. "John Adams," said he, in the hearing of him who has now the honor to address you, "John Adams was our colossus on the floor. Not graceful, not elegant, not always fluent, in his public addresses, he yet came out with a power, both of thought and of expression, which moved us from our seats."

For the part which he was here to perform, Mr. Adams doubtless was eminently fitted. He possessed a bold spirit, which disregarded danger, and a sanguine reliance on the goodness of the cause, and the virtues of the people, which led him to overlook all obstacles. His character, too, had been formed in troubled times. He had been rocked in the early storms of the controversy, and had acquired a decision and a hardihood proportioned to the severity of the discipline which he had undergone.

He not only loved the American cause devoutly, but had studied and understood it. It was all familiar to him. He had tried his powers on the questions which it involved, often and in various ways; and had brought to their consideration whatever of argument or illustration the history of his own country, the history of England, or the stores of ancient or of legal learning could furnish. Every grievance enumerated in the long catalogue of the declaration had been the subject of his discussion, and the object of his remonstrance and reprobation. From 1760, the colonies, the rights of the colonies, the liberties of the colonies, and the wrongs inflicted on the colonies, had engaged his constant attention; and it has surprised those who have had the opportunity of observing, with what full remembrance and with what prompt recollection he could refer, in his extreme old age, to every act of parliament affecting the colonies, distinguishing and stating their respective titles, sections, and provisions; and to all the colonial memorials, remonstrances and petitions with whatever else belonged to the intimate and exact history of the times from that year to 1775. It was, in his own judgment, between these years that the American people came to a full understanding and thorough knowledge of their rights, and to a fixed resolution of maintaining them; and bearing, himself, an active part in all important transactions, the controversy with England being then in effect the business of his life, facts, dates and particulars, made an impression which was never effaced. He was prepared, therefore, by education and discipline, as well as by natural talent and natural temperament, for the part which he was now to act.

The eloquence of Mr. Adams resembled his general character, and formed, indeed, a part of it. It was bold, manly, and energetic, and such the crisis required. When public bodies are to be addressed on momentous occasions, when great interests are at stake, and strong passions excited, nothing is valuable in speech farther than it is connected with high intellectual and moral endowments. Clearness, force, and earnestness, are the qualities which produce conviction. True eloquence, indeed, does not consist in speech. It cannot be brought from far. Labor and learning may toil for it, but they will toil in vain. Words and phrases may be marshaled in every way, but they cannot compass it. It must exist in the man, in the subject, and in the occasion. Affected passion, intense expression, the pomp of declamation, all may aspire after it; they cannot reach it. It comes, if it come at all, like the outbreaking of a fountain from the earth, or the bursting forth of volcanic fires, with spontaneous, original, native force. The graces taught in the schools, the costly ornaments and studied contrivances of speech, shock and disgust men, when their own lives, and the fate of their wives, their children, and their country, hang on the decision of the hour. Then words have lost their power, rhetoric is vain, and all elaborate oratory contemptible. Even genius itself then feels rebuked and subdued, as in the presence of higher qualities. Then patriotism is eloquent; then self-devotion is eloquent. The clear conception, outrunning the deductions of logic, the high purpose, the firm resolve, the dauntless spirit, speaking on the tongue, beaming from the eye, informing every feature, and urging the whole man onward, right onward to his object—this, this is eloquence; or rather it is something greater and higher than all eloquence, it is action, noble, sublime, godlike action.

In July, 1776, the controversy had passed the stage of argument. An appeal had been made to force, and opposing armies were in the field. Congress, then, was to decide whether the tie which had so long bound us to the parent state was to be severed at once, and severed forever. All the colonies had signified their resolution to abide by this decision, and the people looked for it with the most intense anxiety. And surely, fellow-citizens, never, never were men called to a more important political deliberation. If we contemplate it from the point where they then stood, no question could be more full of interest; if we look at it now, and judge of its importance by its effects, it appears in still greater magnitude.

Let us, then, bring before us the assembly, which was about to decide a question thus big with the fate of empire. Let us open their doors and look in upon their deliberations. Let us survey the anxious and care-worn countenances, let us hear the firm-toned voices of this band of patriots.

HANCOCK presides over the solemn sitting; and one of those not yet prepared to pronounce for absolute independence is on the floor, and is urging his reasons for dissenting from the declaration.

"Let us pause! This step once taken, cannot be retraced. This resolution, once passed, will cut off all hope of reconciliation. If success attend the arms of England, we shall then be no longer colonies, with charters and with privileges; these will all be forfeited by this act; and we shall be in the condition of other conquered people, at the mercy of the conquerors. For ourselves, we may be ready to run the hazard; but are we ready to carry the country to that length? Is success so probable as to justify it? Where is the military, where the naval power, by which we are to resist the whole strength of the arm of England, for she will exert that strength to the utmost? Can we rely on the constancy and perseverance of the people? or will they not act as the people of other countries have acted, and, wearied with a long war, submit, in the end, to a worse oppression? While we stand on our old ground, and insist on redress of grievances, we know we are right, and are not answerable for consequences. Nothing, then can be imputed to us. But if we now change our object, carry our pretensions farther, and set up for absolute independence, we shall lose the sympathy of mankind. We shall no longer be defending what we possess, but struggling for something which we never did possess, and which we have solemnly and uniformly disclaimed all intention of pursuing, from the very outset of the troubles. Abandoning thus our old ground, of resistance only to arbitrary acts of oppression, the nations will believe the whole to have been mere pretense, and they will look on us, not as injured, but as ambitious subjects. I shudder before this responsibility. It will be on us, if, relinquishing the ground we have stood on so long, and stood on so safely we now proclaim independence, and carry on the war for that object, while these cities burn, these pleasant fields whiten and bleach with the bones of their owners, and these streams run blood. It will be upon us, it will be upon us, if, failing to maintain this unseasonable and ill-judged declaration, a sterner despotism, maintained by military power, shall be established over our posterity, when we ourselves, given up by an exhausted, a harassed, a misled people, shall have expiated our rashness and atoned for our presumption on the scaffold."

It was for Mr. Adams to reply to arguments like these. We know his opinions, and we know his character. He would commence with his accustomed directness and earnestness.

"'Sink or swim, live or die, survive or perish, I give my hand and my heart to this vote. It is true, indeed, that in the beginning we aimed not at independence. But there's a divinity which shapes our ends. The injustice of England has driven us to arms; and, blinded to her own interest for our good, she has obstinately persisted, till independence is now within our grasp. We have but to reach forth to it, and it is ours. Why, then, should we defer the declaration? Is any man so weak as now to hope for reconciliation with England, which shall leave either safety to the country and its liberties, or safety to his own life and his own honor? Are not you, sir, who sit in that chair, is not he, our venerable colleague near you, are you not both already the proscribed and predestined objects of punishment and of vengeance? Cut off from all hope of royal clemency, what are you, what can you be, while the power of England remains, but outlaws? If we postpone independence, do we mean to carry on, or to give up the war? Do we mean to submit to the measures of parliament, Boston Port Bill and all? Do we mean to submit, and consent that we ourselves shall be ground to powder, and our country and its rights trodden down in the dust? I know we do not mean to submit. We never shall submit. Do we intend to violate that most solemn obligation ever entered into by men, that plighting, before God, of our sacred honor to Washington, when, putting him forth to incur the dangers of war, as well as the political hazards of the times, we promised to adhere to him, in every extremity, with our fortunes and our lives? I know there is not a man here, who would not rather see a general conflagration sweep over the land, or an earthquake sink it, than one jot or title of that plighted faith fall to the ground. For myself, having, twelve months ago, in this place, moved you, that George Washington be appointed commander of the forces raised, or to be raised, for defense of American liberty, may my right hand forget her cunning, and my tongue cleave to the roof of my mouth, if I hesitate or waver in the support I give him.

"The war, then, must go on. We must fight it through. And if the war must go on, why put off longer the declaration of independence? That measure will strengthen us It will give us character abroad. The nations will then treat with us, which they never can do while we acknowledge ourselves subjects, in arms against our sovereign. Nay, I maintain that England herself will sooner treat for peace with us on the footing of independence, than consent, by repealing her acts, to acknowledge that her whole conduct toward us has been a course of injustice and oppression. Her pride will be less wounded by submitting to that course of things which now predestinates our independence, than by yielding the points in controversy to her rebellious subjects. The former she would regard as the result of fortune, the latter she would feel as her own deep disgrace. Why, then, why, then, sir, do we not as soon as possible change this from a civil to a national war? And since we must fight it through, why not put ourselves in a state to enjoy all the benefits of victory, if we gain the victory?

"If we fail, it can be no worse for us. But we shall not fail. The cause will raise up armies; the cause will create navies. The people, the people, if we are true to them, will carry us, and will carry themselves, gloriously, through this struggle. I care not how fickle other people have been found. I know the people of these colonies, and I know that resistance to British aggression is deep and settled in their hearts, and cannot be eradicated. Every colony, indeed, has expressed its willingness to follow, if we but take the lead. Sir, the declaration will inspire the people with increased courage. Instead of a long and bloody war for the restoration of privileges, for redress of grievances, for chartered immunities, held under a British king, set before them the glorious object of entire independence, and it will breathe into them anew the breath of life. Read this declaration at the head of the army; every sword will be drawn from its scabbard, and the solemn vow uttered, to maintain it, or to perish on the bed of honor. Publish it from the pulpit; religion will approve it, and the love of religious liberty will cling round it, resolved to stand with it, or fall with it. Send it to the public halls; proclaim it there; let them hear it who heard the first roar of the enemy's cannon, let them see it who saw their brothers and their sons fall on the field of Bunker Hill, and in the streets of Lexington and Concord, and the very walls will cry out in its support.

"Sir, I know the uncertainty of human affairs, but I see, I see clearly, through this day's business. You and I, indeed, may rue it. We may not live to the time when this declaration shall be made good. We may die; die colonists; die slaves; die, it may be, ignominiously and on the scaffold. Be it so. Be it so. If it be the pleasure of Heaven that my country shall require the poor offering of my life, the victim shall be ready, at the appointed hour of sacrifice, come when that hour may. But while I do live, let me have a country, or at least the hope of a country, and that a free country.

"But whatever may be our fate, be assured, be assured that this declaration will stand. It may cost treasure, and it may cost blood; but it will stand, and it will richly compensate for both. Through the thick gloom of the present I see the brightness of the future as the sun in heaven. We shall make this a glorious, an immortal day. When we are in our graves, our children will honor it. They will celebrate it with thanksgiving, with festivity, with bonfires, and illuminations. On its annual return they will shed tears, copious, gushing tears, not of subjection and slavery, not of agony and distress, but of exultation, of gratitude, and of joy. Sir, before God, I believe the hour is come. My judgment approves this measure, and my whole heart is in it. All that I have, and all that I am, and all that I hope, in this life, I am now ready here to stake upon it; and I leave off as I begun, that live or die, survive or perish, I am for the declaration. It is my living sentiment, and by the blessing of God it shall be my dying sentiment, independence, now, and INDEPENDENCE FOREVER."

And so that day shall be honored, illustrious prophet and patriot! so that day shall be honored, and as often as it returns, thy renown shall come along with it, and the glory of thy life, like the day of thy death, shall not fail from the remembrance of men.

It would be unjust, fellow-citizens, on this occasion while we express our veneration for him who is the immediate subject of these remarks, were we to omit a most respectful, affectionate, and grateful mention of those other great men, his collegues, who stood with him, and with the same spirit, the same devotion, took part in the interesting transaction. Hancock, the proscribed Hancock, exiled from his home by a military governor, cut off by proclamation from the mercy of the crown—Heaven reserved for him the distinguished honor of putting this great question to the vote, and of writing his own name first, and most conspicuously, on that parchment which spoke defiance to the power of the crown of England. There, too, is the name of that other proscribed patriot, Samuel Adams, a man who hungered and thirsted for the independence of his country, who thought the declaration halted and lingered, being himself not only ready, but eager, for it, long before it was proposed: a man of the deepest sagacity, the clearest foresight, and the profoundest judgment in men. And there is Gerry, himself among the earliest and the foremost of the patriots, found, when the battle of Lexington summoned them to common counsels, by the side of Warren, a man who lived to serve his country at home and abroad, and to die in the second place in the government. There, too, is the inflexible, the upright, the Spartan character, Robert Treat Paine. He also lived to serve his country through the struggle, and then withdrew from her councils, only that he might give his labors and his life to his native state, in another relation. These names, fellow-citizens, are the treasures of the commonwealth: and they are treasures which grow brighter by time.

It is now necessary to resume and to finish with great brevity the notice of the lives of those whose virtues and services we have met to commemorate.

Mr. Adams remained in congress from its first meeting till November, 1777, when he was appointed minister to France. He proceeded on that service in the February following, embarking in the Boston frigate on the shore of his native town at the foot of Mount Wollaston. The year following, he was appointed commissioner to treat of peace with England. Returning to the United States, he was a delegate from Braintree in the convention for framing the constitution of this commonwealth, in 1780. At the latter end of the same year, he again went abroad in the diplomatic service of the country, and was employed at various courts, and occupied with various negotiations, until 1788. The particulars of these interesting and important services this occasion does not allow time to relate. In 1782 he concluded our first treaty with Holland. His negotiations with that republic, his efforts to persuade the states-general to recognize our independence, his incessant and indefatigable exertions to represent the American cause favorably on the continent, and to counteract the designs of its enemies, open and secret, and his successful undertaking to obtain loans, on the credit of a nation yet new and unknown, are among his most arduous. most useful, most honorable services. It was his fortune to bear a part in the negotiation for peace with England, and in something more than six years from the declaration which he had so strenuously supported, he had the satisfaction to see the minister plenipotentiary of the crown subscribe to the instrument which declared that his "Britannic majesty acknowledged the United States to be free, sovereign, and independent." In these important transactions, Mr. Adams' conduct received the marked approbation of congress and of the countrty.

While abroad, in 1787, he published his Defense of the American Constitution; a work of merit and ability, though composed with haste, on the spur of a particular occasion, in the midst of other occupations, and under circumstances not admitting of careful revision. The immediate object of the work was to counteract the weight of opinion advanced by several popular European writers of that day, Mr. Turgct, the Abbe de Mably and Dr. Price, at a time when the people of the United States were employed in forming and revising their system of government.

Returning to the United States in 1788, he found the new government about going into operation, and was himself elected the first vice-president, a situation which he filled with reputation for eight years, at the expiration of which he was raised to the presidential chair, as immediate successor to the immortal Washington. In this high station he was succeeded by Mr. Jefferson, after a memorable controversy between their respective friends, in 1801; and from that period his manner of life has been known to all who hear me. He has lived for five-and-twenty years, with every enjoyment that could render old age happy. Not inattentive to the occurrences of the times, political cares have not yet materially, or for any long time, disturbed his repose. In 1820 he acted as elector of president and vice-president, and in the same year we saw him, then at the age of eighty-five, a member of the convention of this commonwealth called to revise the constitution. Forty years before, he had been one of those who formed that constitution; and he had now the pleasure of witnessing that there was little which the people desired to change. Possessing all his faculties to the end of his long life, with an unabated love of reading and contemplation, in the center of interesting circles of friendship and affection, he was blessed in his retirement with whatever of repose and felicity the condition of man allows. He had, also, other enjoyments. He saw around him that prosperity and general happiness which had been the object of his public cares and labors. No man ever beheld more clearly, and for a longer time, the great and beneficial effects of the services rendered by himself to his country. That liberty which he so early defended, that independence of which he was so able an advocate and supporter, he saw, we trust, firmly and securely established. The population of the country thickened around him faster, and extended wider, than his own sanguine predictions had anticipated; and the wealth respectability, and power of the nation sprang up to a magnitude which it is quite impossible he could have expected to witness in his day. He lived also to behold those principles of civil freedom which had been developed, established, and practically applied in America, attract attention, command respect, and awaken imitation, in other regions of the globe; and well might, and well did, he exclaim, "Where will the consequences of the American revolution end?"

If anything yet remains to fill this cup of happiness let it be added that he lived to see a great and intelligent people bestow the highest honor in their gift where he had bestowed his own kindest parental affections and lodged his fondest hopes. Thus honored in life, thus happy at death, he saw the JUBILEE, and he died; and with the last prayers which trembled on his lips was the fervent supplication for his country, "Independence forever!"

Mr. Jefferson, having been occupied in the years 1778 and

1779 in the important service of revising the laws of Virginia, was elected governor of that state, as successor to Patrick Henry, and held the situation when the state was invaded by the British arms. In 1781 he published his Notes on Virginia, a work which attracted attention in Europe as well as America, dispelled many misconceptions respecting this continent, and gave its author a place among men distinguished for science. In November, 1783, he again took his seat in the continental congress, but in the May following was appointed minister plenipotentiary, to act abroad, in the negotiation of commercial treaties, with Dr. Franklin and Mr. Adams. He proceeded to France in execution of this mission, embarking at Boston; and that was the only occasion on which he ever visited this place. In 1785 he was appointed minister to France, the duties of which situation he continued to perform until October, 1789, when he obtained leave to retire, just on the eve of that tremendous revolution which has so much agitated the world in our times. Mr. Jefferson's discharge of his diplomatic duties was marked by great ability, diligence, and patriotism; and while he resided at Paris, in one of the most interesting periods, his character for intelligence, his love of knowledge and of the society of learned men, distinguished him in the highest circles of the French capital. No court in Europe had at that time in Paris a representative commanding or enjoying higher regard for political knowledge or for general attainments, than the minister of this then infant republic. Immediately on his return to his native country, at the organization of the government under the present constitution, his talents and experience recommended him to President Washington for the first office in his gift. He was placed at the head of the department of state. In this situation, also, he manifested conspicuous ability. His correspondence with the ministers of other powers residing here, and his instructions to our own diplomatic agents abroad, are among our ablest state papers. A thorough knowledge of the laws and usages of nations, perfect acquaintance with the immediate subject before him, great felicity, and still greater faculty, in writing, show themselves in whatever effort his official situation called on him to make. It is believed by competent judges, that the diplomatic intercourse of the government of the United States, from the first meeting of the continental congress in 1774 to the present time taken together, would not suffer, in respect to the talent with which it has been conducted, by comparison with anything which other and older states can produce; and to the attainment of this respectability and distinction Mr. Jefferson has contributed his full part.

On the retirement of General Washington from the presidency, and the election of Mr. Adams to that office in 1797, he was chosen vice-president. While presiding in this capacity over the deliberations of the senate, he compiled and published a Manual of Parliamentary Practice, a work of more labor and more merit than is indicated by its size. It is now received as the general standard by which proceedings are regulated; not only in both houses of congress, but in most of the other legislative bodies in the country. In 1801 he was elected president, in opposition to Mr. Adams, and re-elected in 1805, by a vote approaching toward unanimity.

From the time of his final retirement from public life, in 1809, Mr. Jefferson lived as became a wise man. Surrounded by affectionate friends, his ardor in the pursuit of knowledge undiminished, with uncommon health and unbroken spirits, he was able to enjoy largely the rational pleasures of life, and to partake in that public prosperity which he had so much contributed to produce. His kindness and hospitality, the charm of his conversation, the ease of his manners, the extent of his acquirements, and, especially, the full store of revolutionary incidents which he possessed, and which he knew when and how to dispense, rendered his abode in a high degree attractive to his admiring countrymen, while his high public and scientific character drew toward him every intelligent and educated traveler from abroad. Both Mr. Adams and Mr. Jefferson had the pleasure of knowing that the respect which they so largely received was not paid to their official stations. They were not men made great by office; but great men, on whom the country for its own benefit had conferred office. There was that in them which office did not give, and which the relinquishment of office did not, and could not, take away. In their retirement, in the midst of their fellow-citizens, themselves private citizens, they enjoyed as high regard and esteem as when filling the most important places of public trust. There remained to Mr. Jefferson yet one other work of patriotism and beneficence, the establishment of a university in his native state. To this object he devoted years of incessant and anxious attention, and by the enlightened liberality of the legislature of Virginia, and the cooperation of other able and zealous friends, he lived to see it accomplished. May all success attend this infant seminary; and may those who enjoy its advantages, as often as their eyes shall rest on the neighboring height, recollect what they owe to their disinterested and indefatigable benefactor; and may letters honor him who thus labored in the cause of letters!

Thus useful, and thus respected, passed the old age of Thomas Jefferson. But time was on its ever-ceaseless wing, and was now bringing the last hour of this illustrious man. He saw its approach with undisturbed serenity. He counted the moments as they passed, and beheld that his last sands were falling. That day, too, was at hand which he had helped to make immortal. One wish, one hope, if it were not presumptuous, beat in his fainting breast. Could it be so might it please God, he would desire once more to see the sun, once more to look abroad on the scene around him on the great day of liberty. Heaven, in its mercy, fulfilled that prayer. He saw that sun, he enjoyed its sacred light he thanked God for this mercy, and bowed his aged head to the grave. "Felix, non vitae tantum claritate, sid etiam opportunitate mortis."

The last public labor of Mr. Jefferson naturally suggests the expression of the high praise which is due, both to him and to Mr. Adams, for their uniform and zealous attachment to learning, and to the cause of general knowledge. Of the advantages of learning, indeed, and of literary accomplishments, their own characters were striking recommendations and illustrations. They were scholars, ripe and good scholars; widely acquainted with ancient, as well as modern literature, and not altogether uninstructed in the deeper sciences. Their acquirements, doubtless, were different, and so were the particular objects of their literary pursuits; as their tastes and characters, in these respects differed like those of other men. Being, also, men of busy lives, with great objects requiring action constantly before them, their attainments in letters did not become showy or obtrusive. Yet I would hazard the opinion, that, if we could now ascertain all the causes which gave them eminence, and distinction in the midst of the great men with whom they acted, we should find not among the least their early acquisitions in literature, the resources which it furnished, the promptitude and facility which it communicated, and the wide field it opened for analogy and illustration; giving them thus, on every subject, a larger view and a broader range, as well for discussion as for the government of their own conduct.

Literature sometimes, and pretensions to it much oftener disgusts, by appearing to hang loosely on the character, like something foreign or extraneous, not a part, but an ill-adjusted appendage; or by seeming to overload and weigh it down by its unsightly bulk, like the productions of bad taste in architecture, where there is messy and cumbrous ornament without strength or solidity of column. This has exposed learning, and especially classical learning, to reproach. Men have seen that it might exist without mental superiority, without vigor, without good taste, and without utility. But in such cases classical learning has only not inspired natural talent, or, at most, it has but made original feebleness of intellect, and natural bluntness of perception, something more conspicuous. The question, after all, if it be a question, is, whether literature, ancient as well as modern, does not assist a good understanding, improve natural good taste, add polished armor to native strength, and render its possessor, not only more capable of deriving private happiness from contemplation and reflection, but more accomplished also for action in the affairs of life, and especially for public action. Those whose memories we now honor were learned men; but their learning was kept in its proper place, and made subservient to the uses and objects of life. They were scholars, not common nor superficial; but their scholarship was so in keeping with their character, so blended and inwrought, that careless observers, or bad judges, not seeing an ostentatious display of it, might infer that it did not exist; forgetting, or not knowing, that classical learning in men who act in conspicuous public stations, perform duties which exercise the faculty of writing, or address popular deliberative, or judicial bodies, is often felt where it is little seen, and sometimes felt more effectually because it is not seen at all.

But the cause of knowledge, in a more enlarged sense, the cause of general knowledge and of a popular education, had no warmer friends, nor more powerful advocates, than Mr. Adams and Mr. Jefferson. On this foundation they knew the whole republican system rested; and this great and all-important truth they strove to impress, by all the means in their power. In the early publication already referred to Mr. Adams expresses the strong and just sentiment, that the education of the poor is more important, even to the rich themselves, than all their own. On this great truth indeed, is founded that unrivaled, that invaluable political and moral institution, our own blessing and the glory of our fathers, the New England system of free schools.

As the promotion of knowledge had been the object of their regard through life, so these great men made it the subject of their testamentary bounty. Mr. Jefferson is understood to have bequeathed his library to the university of his native state, and that of Mr. Adams is bestowed on the inhabitants of Quincy.

Mr. Adams and Mr. Jefferson, fellow-citizens, were successively presidents of the United States. The comparative merits of their respective administrations for a long time agitated and divided public opinion. They were rivals, each supported by numerous and powerful portions of the people, for the highest office. This contest, partly the cause and partly the consequence of the long existence of two great political parties in the country, is now part of the history of our government. We may naturally regret that anything should have occurred to create difference and discord between those who had acted harmoniously and efficiently in the great concerns of the revolution. But this is not the time, nor this the occasion, for entering into the grounds of that difference, or for attempting to discuss the merits of the questions which it involves. As practical questions, they were canvassed when the measures which they regarded were acted on and adopted; and as belonging to history, the time has not come for their consideration.

It is, perhaps, not wonderful, that, when the constitution of the United States went first into operation, different opinions should be entertained as to the extent of the powers conferred by it. Here was a natural source of diversity of sentiment. It is still less wonderful, that that event, about cotemporary with our government under the present constitution, which so entirely shocked all Europe, and disturbed our relations with her leading powers, should be thought, by different men, to have different bearings on our own prosperity; and that the early measures adopted by our government, in consequence of this new state of things, should be seen in opposite lights. It is for the future historian, when what now remains of prejudice and misconception shall have passed away, to state these different opinions, and pronounce impartial judgment. In the mean time, all good men rejoice, and well may rejoice, that the sharpest differences sprung out of measures which, whether right or wrong, have ceased with the exigencies that gave them birth, and have left no permanent effect, either on the constitution or on the general prosperity of the country. This remark, I am aware, may be supposed to have its exception in one measure, the alteration of the constitution as to the mode of choosing President; but it is true in its general application. Thus the course of policy pursued toward France in 1798, on the one hand, and the measures of commercial restriction commenced in 1807, on the other, both subjects of warm and severe opposition, have passed away and left nothing behind them. They were temporary, and whether wise or unwise, their consequences were limited to their respective occasions. It is equally clear, at the same time, and it is equally gratifying, that those measures of both administrations which were of durable importance, and which drew after them interesting and long remaining consequences, have received general approbation. Such was the organization, or rather the creation, of the navy, in the administration of Mr. Adams; such the acquisition of Louisiana, in that of Mr. Jefferson. The country, it may safely be added, is not likely to be willing either to approve, or to reprobate, indiscriminately, and in the aggregate, all the measures of either, or of any, administration. The dictate of reason and justice is, that, holding each one his own sentiments on the points in difference, we imitate the great men themselves in the forbearance and moderation which they have cherished, and in the mutual respect and kindness which they have been so much inclined to feel and to reciprocate.

No men, fellow-citizens, ever served their country with more entire exemption from every imputation of selfish and mercenary motives, than those to whose memory we are paying these proofs of respect. A suspicion of any disposition to enrich themselves, or to profit by their public employments, never rested on either. No sordid motive approached them. The inheritance which they have left to their children is of their character and their fame.

Fellow-citizens, I will detain you no longer by this faint and feeble tribute to the memory of the illustrious dead. Even in other hands, adequate justice could not be performed, within the limits of this occasion. Their highest, their best praise, is your deep conviction of their merits, your affectionate gratitude for their labors and services. It is not my voice, it is this cessation of ordinary pursuits, this arresting of all attention, these solemn ceremonies, and this crowded house, which speak their eulogy. Their fame, indeed, is safe. That is now treasured up beyond the reach of accident. Although no sculptured marble should rise to their memory, nor engraved stone bear record of their deeds, yet will their remembrance be as lasting as the land they honored. Marble columns may, indeed, moulder into dust, time may erase all impress from the crumbling stone, but their fame remains; for with

AMERICAN LIBERTY it rose, and with AMERICAN LIBERTY ONLY can it perish. It was the last swelling peal of yonder choir, THEIR BODIES ARE BURIED IN PEACE, BUT THEIR NAME LIVETH EVERMORE. I catch that solemn song, I echo that lofty strain of funeral triumph, THEIR NAME LIVETH EVERMORE.

Of the illustrious signers of the declaration of independence there now remains only Charles Carroll. He seems an aged oak, standing alone on the plain, which time has spared a little longer after all its cotemporaries have been leveled with the dust. Venerable object! we delight to gather round its trunk, while yet it stands, and to dwell beneath its shadow. Sole survivor of an assembly of as great men as the world has witnessed, in a transaction one of the most important that history records, what thoughts, what interesting reflections, must fill his elevated and devout soul! If he dwell on the past, how touching its recollections; if he survey the present, how happy, how joyous, how full of the fruition of that hope, which his ardent patriotism indulged; if he glance at the future, how does the prospect of his country's advancement almost bewilder his weakened conception! Fortunate, distinguished patriot! Interesting relic of the past! Let him know that, while we honor the dead, we do not forget the living; and that there is not a heart here which does not fervently pray that Heaven may keep him yet back from the society of his companions.

And now, fellow-citizens, let us not retire from this occasion without a deep and solemn conviction of the duties which have devolved upon us. This lovely land, this glorious liberty, these benign institutions, the dear purchase of our fathers, are ours; ours to enjoy, ours to preserve, ours to transmit. Generations past and generations to come hold us responsible for this sacred trust. Our fathers, from behind, admonish us, with their anxious paternal voices; posterity calls out to us, from the bosom of the future; the world turns hither its solicitous eyes; all, all conjure us to act wisely, and faithfully, in the relation which we sustain. We can never, indeed, pay the debt which is upon us; but by virtue, by morality, by religion, by the cultivation of every good principle and every good habit, we may hope to enjoy the blessing, through our day, and to leave it unimpared to our children. Let us feel deeply how much of what we are and of what we possess we owe to this liberty, and to these institutions of government. Nature has indeed given us a soil which yields bounteously to the hands of industry, the mighty and fruitful ocean is before us, and the skies over our heads shed health and vigor. But what are lands, and seas, and skies to civilized man, without society, without knowledge, without morals, without religious culture; and how can these be enjoyed, in all their extent and all their excellence, but under the protection of wise institutions and a free government? Fellow-citizens, there is not one of us, there is not one of us here present, who does not, at this moment, and at every moment, experience in his own condition, and in the condition of those most near and dear to him, the influence and the benefits of this liberty and these institutions. Let us then acknowledge the blessing, let us feel it deeply and powerfully, let us cherish a strong affection for it, and resolve to maintain and perpetuate it. The blood of our fathers, let it not have been shed in vain; the great hope of posterity, let it not be blasted.

The striking attitude, too, in which we stand to the world around us, a topic to which, I fear, I advert too often, and dwell on too long, cannot be altogether omitted here. Neither individuals nor nations can perform their part well, until they understand and feel its importance, and comprehend and justly appreciate all the duties belonging to it. It is not to inflate national vanity, nor to swell a light and empty feeling of self-importance, but it is that we may judge justly of our situation, and of our own duties, that I earnestly urge this consideration of our position and our character among the nations of the earth. It cannot be denied, but by those who would dispute against the sun, that with America, and in America, a new era commences in human affairs. This era is distinguished by free representative governments, by entire religious liberty, by improved systems of national intercourse, by a newly awakened and unconquerable spirit of free inquiry and by a diffusion of knowledge through the community, such as has been before altogether unknown and unheard of. America, America, our country, fellow-citizens, our own dear and native land, is inseparably connected, fast bound up, in fortune and by fate, with these great interests. If they fall, we fall with them; if they stand, it will be because we have upholden them. Let us contemplate, then, this connection, which binds the prosperity of others to our own; and let us manfully discharge all the duties which it imposes. If we cherish the virtues and principles of our fathers, Heaven will assist us to carry on the work of human liberty and human happiness. Auspicious omens cheer us. Great examples are before us. Our own firmament now shines brightly upon our path. WASHINGTON is in the clear, upper sky. These other stars have now joined the American constellation; they circle round their center, and the heavens beam with new light. Beneath this illumination let us walk the course of life, and at its close devoutly commend our beloved country, the common parent of us all, to the Divine Benignity.

*Extract of a letter written by John Adams, dated at Worcester, Massachusetts, October 12, 1755.

"Soon after the Reformation, a few people came over into this New World, for conscience' sake. Perhaps this apparently trivial incident may transfer the great seat of empire into America. It looks likely to me; for, if we can remove the turbulent Gallios, our people, according to the exactest computations, will, in another century, become more numerous than England itself. Should this be the case, since we have, I may say, all the naval stores of the nation in our hands, it will be easy to obtain a mastery of the seas; and then the united forces of all Europe will not be able to subdue us. The only way to keep us from setting up for ourselves is to disunite us.

"Be not surprised that I am turned polititian. The whole town is immersed in politics. The interests of nations, and all the dira of war, make the subject of every conversation. I sit and hear, and after having been led through a maze of sage obversations, I sometimes retire, and, laying things together, form some reflections pleasing to myself. The produce of one of these reveries you have read above."

**This question. of the power of parliament over the colonies, was discussed with singular ability by Governor Hutchinson on the one side, and the house of representatives of Massachusetts on the other, in 1773. The argument of the house is in the form of an answer to the governor's message, and was reported by Mr. Samuel Adams, Mr. Hancock, Mr. Hawley, Mr. Bowers, Mr. Hobson, Mr. Foster, Mr. Phillips and Mr. Thayer. As the power of the parliament had been acknowledged, so far, at least, as to affect us by laws of trade, it was not easy to settle the line of distinction. It was thought, however, to be very clear that the charters of the colonies had exempted them from the general legislation of the British parliament. See Massachusetts State Papers, p. 351

THE STORY OF JEFFERSON
FOR A SCHOOL OR CLUB PROGRAMME

Each numbered paragraph is to be given to a pupil or member to read, or to recite in a clear, distinct tone.

If the school or club is small, each person may take three or four paragraphs, but should not be required to recite them in succession.

1. Thomas Jefferson was born April 13, 1743. His home was among the mountains of Central Virginia on a farm, called Shadwell, 150 miles northwest of Williamsburg.

2. His father's name was Peter Jefferson. His ancestors were Welsh people. Like George Washington, he learned the art of surveying. He was a superb specimen of a Virginia landholder, being a giant in frame, and having the strength of three strong men.

3. One of his father's favorite maxims was, "Never ask another to do for you what you can do for yourself."

4. His mother's name was Jane Randolph. She was a noble woman. Thomas Jefferson derived his temper, his disposition, his sympathy with living nature from his mother.

5. He was very fond of the violin, as were a great many of the Virginia people. During twelve years of his life, he practiced on that instrument three hours a day.

6. He early learned to love the Indians from his acquaintance with many of their best chiefs. He held them in great regard during his life.

7. His father died in 1757, when Thomas was but fourteen years of age. The son always spoke of his father with pride and veneration.

8. He entered William and Mary College in the spring of 1760, when he was seventeen years old.

9. After two years of college life he began the study of law in 1763.

10. When he came of age in April, 1764, he signalized the event by planting a beautiful avenue of trees near his house.

11. While studying law he carried on the business of a farmer, and showed by his example, that the genuine culture of the mind is the best preparation for the common, as well as the higher, duties of life.

12. When he was elected to the Virginia Assembly, and thus entered upon the public service, he avowed afterwards to Madison, that "the esteem of the world was, perhaps, of higher value in his eyes than everything in it."

13. His marriage was a very happy one. His wife was a beautiful woman, her countenance being brilliant with color and expression.

14. Six children blessed their marriage, five girls and a boy. Only two of them, Martha and Mary, lived to mature life.

15. Monticello, the home of Jefferson, was blessed at every period of his long life with a swarm of merry children whom, although not his own, he greatly loved.

16. Mrs. Jefferson once said of her husband, who had done a

generous deed for which he had received an ungrateful return, "He is so good himself that he cannot understand how bad other people may be."

17. In his draft of instructions for Virginia's delegates to the Congress which was to meet in Philadelphia in September, 1774, he used some plain language to George III.

18. The stupid, self-willed and conceited monarch did not follow his advice, and so lost the American Colonies, the brightest jewels in England's crown.

19. Sixty gentlemen, in silk stockings and pigtails, sitting in a room of no great size in a plain brick building up a narrow alley in Philadelphia, composed the Continental Congress.

20. Thomas Jefferson was one of the members most welcome in that body. He brought with him "a reputation," as John Adams records, "for literature, science, and a happy talent for composition."

21. As late as Nov. 29, 1775, Jefferson clung to the idea of connection with great Britain.

22. He wrote his kinsman, John Randolph, that there was not a man in the British Empire who more cordially loved a union with Great Britain than he did.

23. He said: "It is an immense misfortune to the whole empire to have such a king at such a time. We are told, and everything proves it true, that he is the bitterest enemy we have."

24. When the draft of the Declaration was submitted to the Congress it made eighteen suppressions, six additions and ten alterations; and nearly every one was an improvement.

25. It should be a comfort to students who have to witness the corrections of their compositions to know, that this great work of Jefferson, which has given him immortal fame had to be

pruned of its crudities, redundancies and imprudences.

26. They should be as ready as he was to submit to criticisms and to profit by them as he did, in their future efforts.

27. Daniel Webster shall tell in his own language the remainder of this story of Jefferson's life.

28. "In 1781 he published his notes on Virginia, a work which attracted attention in Europe as well as America, dispelled many misconceptions respecting this continent, and gave its author a place among men distinguished for science.

29. "With Dr. Franklin and Mr. Adams, in 1784, he proceeded to France, in execution of his mission as Minister plenipotentiary, to act in the negotiation of commercial treaties.

30. "In 1785 he was appointed Minister to France.

31. "Mr. Jefferson's discharge of his diplomatic duties was marked by great ability, diligence and patriotism.

32. "While he resided in Paris, in one of the most interesting periods, his love of knowledge, and of the society of learned men, distinguished him in the highest circles of the French capital.

33. "Immediately on his return to his native country he was placed by Washington at the head of the department of State.

34. "In this situation, also, he manifested conspicuous ability.

35. "His correspondence with the ministers of other powers residing here, and his instructions to our own diplomatic agents abroad are among our ablest State papers.

36. "In 1797 he was chosen Vice President. In 1801 he was elected President in opposition to Mr. Adams, and reelected in

1805, by a vote approaching towards unanimity.

37. "From the time of his final retirement from public life Mr. Jefferson lived as becomes a wise man.

38. "Surrounded by affectionate friends, his ardor in the pursuit of knowledge undiminished, with uncommon health and unbroken spirits, he was able to enjoy largely the rational pleasures of life, and to partake in that public prosperity which he had so much contributed to produce.

39. "His kindness and hospitality, the charm of his conversation, the ease of his manners, and especially the full store of revolutionary incidents which he possessed, and which he knew when and how to dispense, rendered his abode in a high degree attractive to his admiring countrymen.

40. "His high public and scientific character drew towards him every intelligent and educated traveler from abroad.

41. "Both Mr. Adams and Mr. Jefferson had the pleasure of knowing that the respect which they so largely received was not paid to their official stations.

42. "They were not men made great by office; but great men, on whom the country for its own benefit had conferred office.

43. "There was that in them which office did not give, and which the relinquishment of office did not and could not take away.

44. "In their retirement, in the midst of their fellow citizens, themselves private citizens, they enjoyed as high regard and esteem as when filling the most important places of public trust.

45. "Thus useful and thus respected passed the old age of Thomas Jefferson.

46. "But time was on its ever-ceaseless wing, and was now bringing the last hour of this illustrious man.

47. "He saw its approach with undisturbed serenity. He counted the moments as they passed, and beheld that his last sands were falling.

48. "That day, too, was at hand which he had helped make immortal. One wish, one hope—if it were not presumptuous—beat in his fainting breast.

49. "Could it be so - might it please God—he would desire once more to see the sun—once more to look abroad on the scene around him, on the great day of liberty.

50. "Heaven in its mercy fulfilled that prayer. He saw that sun—he enjoyed that sacred light—he thanked God for this mercy, and bowed his aged head to the grave."

PROGRAMME FOR A JEFFERSONIAN EVENING

1. Vocal Solo—"Star Spangled Banner."

2. Recitation—One of Jefferson's Speeches.

3. Description of Jefferson's Home, Illustrated by Pictures.

4. Recitation—Declaration of Independence.

5. Recitation—"Battle of the Kegs," by Francis Hopkinson, ("Progress," Vol. 2, page 761).

6. Instrumental Music—"Yankee Doodle."

7. Home Life of the Statesman. (Paper or Address.)

8. Anecdotes of Jefferson.

9. Question Box Concerning the Politics of the Time.

10. Vocal Solo—"My Country, 'Tis of Thee."

QUESTONS FOR REVIEW

When and where was Thomas Jefferson born? What was his height? What was the color of his hair and eyes? What can you say of his literary ability? What of his scholarship? What of his moral character? To which of his teachers was he especially indebted? When was his public career begun? What resolution was then taken? What effect would this resolution have upon modern politicians, if it were made and faithfully kept? Upon what subject was his first important speech made? With what result? Whom did Jefferson marry? What was the reception given Jefferson and his bride? What important public document did he prepare in connection with the Revolution? When did he take his seat in Congress? In what way was he connected with the Declaration of Independence? Who were his associates on the Committee? Give a brief history of the events connected with the signing of the Declaration of Independence? How much time passed before the Articles of Confederation were formally signed by the States? What were the overt acts of opposition by the various States? What was the Alien act? What was the Sedition act? What instances can you give of the prompt punishment of seditious utterances? When were the Alien and Sedition acts repealed? What important measures did Jefferson succeed in passing in his own State? When did he become Governor of the State? What were his duties in relation to foreign treaties? What were his impressions concerning the French government? What was his influence upon educational work? What was the character of the Barbary States? Why were they permitted to hold Americans as captives? What was Jefferson's opinion on the subject? When did he enter Washington's Cabinet, and what position did he fill? What was his relation to Alexander Hamilton? Who were the other members of the Cabinet? What led Jefferson to resign from the Cabinet? When did he become Vice President? How did President Adams treat him? What have you to say about Jefferson's "Manual of Parliamentary Practice?" Who were the Federal nominees for President and Vice President in 1800? What was the note of alarm sounded by Hamilton? What was the attitude of the clergy towards Jefferson, and why? Who were the Federalists? Who were the Republicans? What name did the Republicans afterwards take? What were some of the exciting incidents connected with the vote for President? What was the number of ballots cast for President? Who was the Vice President elected with Jefferson? What was the character of his administration? Who were the members of his Cabinet? Did Jefferson turn men in a wholesale way out of office? What was his attitude towards ceremonies? How did he dress? When was he re-elected? What was the most important result of his influence? What great purchase of territory was made? What States and Territories have been carved out of it? Who explored the upper Missouri and Columbia River country, and when? What steamboat made her maiden trip, and when? When was the first boat load of anthracite coal shipped to Philadelphia? What pirates were snuffed out, and when? Why did John Quincy Adams resign his seat in the United States Senate? What was the Non-Intercourse act? What was the condition of our commerce at this time? What Act proved to be one of his greatest mistakes? When was it passed? When repealed? What was his financial condition? What were the results of his efforts for education? What did Congress pay for his library? When did he die? Who died on the same day that Jefferson did? What did Horace Greeley say about the coincidence? What was the character of Jefferson as a slaveholder? Why is there a difference in Jefferson's portraits? What was Daniel Webster's statement regarding, his countenance? What was his opinion of slavery? What was Jefferson's opinion concerning happiness? What did he say of resignations? What is the epitaph on Jefferson's tomb? What was Jefferson's statement regarding promises for the Presidency? What is the story of the Mould Board of Least Resistance? What is the story of Jefferson as an inventor? What is the story of Jefferson and the horse jockey? What was the peculiar relationship between Jefferson and Patrick Henry? Who were some of the brilliant members of the Virginia assembly? What are the main features of Henry's famous speech before that assembly? What were the treasures Jefferson bequeathed to his country and his State? What did Jefferson say of titles of honor and office? What was his opinion of a third term? What were his views regarding lawyers in Congress? What is the true history of the Mecklenburg Declarations of Independence? What were Jefferson's oratorical powers?

SUBJECTS FOR SPECIAL STUDY

1. The Declaration of Independence as a literary production.

2. The Declaration of Independence as apparently founded in Acts xvii, 26.

3. General condition of the Country at the time of Jefferson's election to the Presidency.

4. Leading events connected with his administration.

5. General results of his political influence.

6. Leading characteristics of the man.

7. Jefferson and Hamilton. Littell's Age, Vol. 81, p. 613.

8. College Days of Jefferson. Atlantic Monthly, Vol. 29, p, 16.

9. Family of Jefferson. Harpers Mag., Vol. 43, p. 366.

10. Jefferson in Continental Congress. Atlantic Monthly, Vol. 29, p. 676.

11. Jefferson in the War of the Revolution. Atlantic Monthly, Vol. 29, p. 517.

12. Jefferson and nullification. See Lives of Jefferson.

13. Jefferson and Patrick Henry. See Lives of Jefferson..

14. Pecuniary Embarrassments of Thomas Jefferson. See Lives of Jefferson.

15. Religious Opinions of Jefferson. See Lives of Jefferson.

16. Jefferson a Reformer of Old Virginia. Atlantic Monthly Vol 30, p. 32

BIBLIOGRAPHY

For those who wish to read extensively, the following works are especially commended:

Life of Thomas Jefferson. By James Parton. Jas. R. Osgood & Co., Boston, 1874.

Life of Thomas Jefferson. By Henry S. Randall, LL. D. J. B. Lippincott & Co., Philadelphia.

Life of Thomas Jefferson. John Robert Irelan, M. D., Chicago.

Autobiography of Thomas Jefferson.

Thomas Jefferson, the Man of Letters. Lewis Henry Routell, Chicago. Privately printed.

Biography of Thomas Jefferson. Cyclopedia of American Biography. D. Appleton & Co.

History of the People of the United States. John Bach McMaster. Vols. I and II. D. Appleton & Co.

Lives of the Presidents. John Frost, LL. D. Phillips & Sampson, Boston.

Eulogy on Adams and Jefferson. Daniel Webster, Faneuil Hall, Aug. 2, 1826.

Character of Thomas Jefferson. North American Review, Vol. 91, p. 107.

Jefferson's Opinions on Slavery. Andrew D. White, Atlantic Mag., Vol. 9, p. 29.

Jefferson and Alexander Hamilton. Littell's Living Age. Vol. 81, p. 273.

War of Independence. John Fiske. Houghton, Mifflin & Co., Boston and New York.

The Critical Period of American History. John Fiske. Houghton, Mifflin & Co., Boston and New Yorok.[sic]

CHRONOLOGICAL EVENTS In the Life of Jefferson

1743 Born Albemarle County, Virginia, April 2.

1760 Entered William and Mary College.

1764 Admitted to the bar of the General Court of Virginia when 21 years of age.

1769 Chosen Representative in the Provincial Legislature.

1772 Married Mrs. Martha Skelton, January 21st.

1773 Appointed Member of the First Committee of Correspondence established by the Colonial Legislature, March 12th.

1774 Published the "Summary View of the Rights of British America."

1776 Chosen to a Seat in the Continental Congress. Appointed Chairman of the Committee to prepare the Declaration of Independence.

1779 Elected to the Virginia Legislature. Helped alleviate the condition of the British Prisoners sent from Saratoga to Charlottesville, Va. Elected by the Legislature to succeed Patrick Henry as Governor of Virginia, June 1.

1781 Elected to the Legislature of Virginia after serving as

Governor two years. "Notes of Virginia" written.

1782 Appointed by Congress to serve with the American Negotiators for Peace.

1783 Elected Delegate to Congress. Wrote Notes on the Establishment of a Coinage of the United States.

1784 Appointed by Congress as Minister Plenipotentiary, with John Adams and Benjamin Franklin, to negotiate Treaties of Commerce with Foreign Nations, May.

1785 Succeeded Franklin as Minister to France.

1789 Appointed Secretary of State by Washington.

1793 Resigned the position of Secretary of State, December 31.

1796 Elected Vice-President of the United States.

1800 Eletced [sic] President of the Untied States.

1803 Louisiana Purchase.

1804 Northwestern Exploring Expedition under Lewis and Clark. Re-Elected President of the United States.

1807 Passage of The Embargo Act, December 22.

1818 University of Virginia founded, of which Jefferson was Rector until his death.

1826 Died on the same day that John Adams expired, July 4th.

Choose from Thousands of 1stWorldLibrary Classics By

Adolphus WilliamWard
Aesop
Agatha Christie
Alexander Aaronsohn
Alexander Kielland
Alexandre Dumas
Alfred Gatty
Alfred Ollivant
Alice Duer Miller
Alice Turner Curtis
Alice Dunbar
Ambrose Bierce
Amelia E. Barr
Andrew Lang
Andrew McFarland Davis
Anna Sewell
Annie Besant
Annie Hamilton Donnell
Annie Payson Call
Anton Chekhov
Arnold Bennett
Arthur Conan Doyle
Arthur Ransome
Atticus
B. M. Bower
Basil King
Bayard Taylor
Ben Macomber
Booth Tarkington
Bram Stoker
C. Collodi
C. E. Orr
C. M. Ingleby
Carolyn Wells
Catherine Parr Traill
Charles A. Eastman
Charles Dickens
Charles Dudley Warner
Charles Farrar Browne
Charles Ives
Charles Kingsley
Charles Lathrop Pack
Charles Whibley
Charles Willing Beale
Charlotte M. Braeme
Charlotte M.Yonge
Clair W. Hayes
Clarence Day Jr.
Clarence E. Mulford

Clemence Housman
Confucius
Cornelis DeWitt Wilcox
Cyril Burleigh
D. H. Lawrence
Daniel Defoe
David Garnett
Don Carlos Janes
Donald Keyhole
Dorothy Kilner
Dougan Clark
E. Nesbit
E.P.Roe
E. Phillips Oppenheim
Edgar Allan Poe
Edgar Rice Burroughs
Edith Wharton
Edward J. O'Biren
John Cournos
Edwin L. Arnold
Eleanor Atkins
Elizabeth Cleghorn Gaskell
Elizabeth Von Arnim
Ellem Key
Emily Dickinson
Erasmus W. Jones
Ernie Howard Pie
Ethel Turner
Ethel Watts Mumford
Eugenie Foa
Eugene Wood
Evelyn Everett-Green
Everard Cotes
F. J. Cross
Federick Austin Ogg
Ferdinand Ossendowski
Francis Bacon
Francis Darwin
Frances Hodgson Burnett
Frank Gee Patchin
Frank Harris
Frank Jewett Mather
Frank L. Packard
Frederick Trevor Hill
Frederick Winslow Taylor
Friedrich Kerst
Friedrich Nietzsche
Fyodor Dostoyevsky

Gabrielle E. Jackson
Garrett P. Serviss
Gaston Leroux
George Ade
Geroge Bernard Shaw
George Ebers
George Eliot
George MacDonald
George Orwell
George Tucker
George W. Cable
George Wharton James
Gertrude Atherton
Grace E. King
Grant Allen
Guillermo A. Sherwell
Gulielma Zollinger
Gustav Flaubert
H. A. Cody
H. B. Irving
H. G. Wells
H. H. Munro
H. Irving Hancock
H. Rider Haggard
H. W. C. Davis
Hamilton Wright Mabie
Hans Christian Andersen
Harold Avery
Harold McGrath
Harriet Beecher Stowe
Harry Houidini
Helent Hunt Jackson
Helen Nicolay
Hendy David Thoreau
Henrik Ibsen
Henry Adams
Henry Ford
Henry Frost
Henry James
Henry Jones Ford
Henry Seton Merriman
Henry Wadsworth Longfellow
Henry W Longfellow
Herbert A. Giles
Herbert N. Casson
Herman Hesse
Homer
Honore De Balzac

Horace Walpole	Laurence Housman	Robert Lansing
Horatio Alger, Jr.	Leo Tolstoy	Robert Michael Ballantyne
Howard Pyle	Leonid Andreyev	Robert W. Chambers
Howard R. Garis	Lewis Carroll	Rosa Nouchette Carey
Hugh Lofting	Lilian Bell	Ross Kay
Hugh Walpole	Lloyd Osbourne	Rudyard Kipling
Humphry Ward	Louis Tracy	Samuel B. Allison
Ian Maclaren	Louisa May Alcott	Samuel Hopkins Adams
Israel Abrahams	Lucy Fitch Perkins	Sarah Bernhardt
J.G.Austin	Lucy Maud Montgomery	Selma Lagerlof
J. Henri Fabre	Lydia Miller Middleton	Sherwood Anderson
J. M. Barrie	Lyndon Orr	Sigmund Freud
J. Macdonald Oxley	M. H. Adams	Standish O'Grady
J. S. Knowles	Margaret E. Sangster	Stanley Weyman
J. Storer Clouston	Margaret Vandercook	Stella Benson
Jack London	Maria Edgeworth	Stephen Crane
Jacob Abbott	Maria Thompson Daviess	Stewart Edward White
James Allen	Mariano Azuela	Stijn Streuvels
James Lane Allen	Marion Polk Angellotti	Swami Abhedananda
James Andrews	Mark Overton	Swami Parmananda
James Baldwin	Mark Twain	T. S. Ackland
James DeMille	Mary Austin	The Princess Der Ling
James Joyce	Mary Cole	Thomas A. Janvier
James Oliver Curwood	Mary Rowlandson	Thomas A Kempis
James Oppenheim	Mary Wollstonecraft	Thomas Anderton
James Otis	Shelley	Thomas Bailey Aldrich
Jane Austen	Max Beerbohm	Thomas Bulfinch
Jens Peter Jacobsen	Myra Kelly	Thomas De Quincey
Jerome K. Jerome	Nathaniel Hawthrone	Thomas H. Huxley
John Burroughs	O. F. Walton	Thomas Hardy
John F. Kennedy	Oscar Wilde	Thomas More
John Gay	Owen Johnson	Thornton W. Burgess
John Glasworthy	P.G.Wodehouse	U. S. Grant
John Habberton	Paul and Mable Thorn	Valentine Williams
John Joy Bell	Paul G. Tomlinson	Victor Appleton
John Milton	Paul Severing	Virginia Woolf
John Philip Sousa	Peter B. Kyne	Walter Scott
Jonathan Swift	Plato	Washington Irving
Joseph Carey	R. Derby Holmes	Wilbur Lawton
Joseph Conrad	R. L. Stevenson	Wilkie Collins
Joseph Jacobs	Rabindranath Tagore	Willa Cather
Julian Hawthrone	Rahul Alvares	Willard F. Baker
Julies Vernes	Ralph Waldo Emmerson	William Makepeace Thackeray
Justin Huntly McCarthy	Rene Descartes	William W. Walter
Kakuzo Okakura	Rex E. Beach	Winston Churchill
Kenneth Grahame	Richard Harding Davis	Yei Theodora Ozaki
Kate Langley Bosher	Richard Jefferies	Young E. Allison
L. A. Abbot	Robert Barr	Zane Grey
L. T. Meade	Robert Frost	
L. Frank Baum	Robert Gordon Anderson	
Laura Lee Hope	Robert L. Drake